DECLARE

UNLEASH GREATNESS THROUGH MENTAL FITNESS

A Greatness Realized Series

WELCOME SARAH

DECLARE
©2019 by Welcome Sarah

A Greatness Realized Series

All rights reserved. No part of this book may be reproduced or
transmitted in any form or by any means, electronic or mechanical,
including photocopying and recording, or by any information storage
and retrieval system without permission.

All definitions, unless otherwise indicated, are taken from Merriam-
Webster Dictionary®. Copyright © 2016 by Merriam-Webster, Inc.

First Edition: August 2019

Printed in the United States of America

Cover Design by Aaron Escamilla
Edited by Amy Noelck

For my mom.

You are the most amazingly, ridiculous representation of greatness that I have ever had the privilege to experience and encounter. You are the embodiment of mental fitness, resilience, and grace. Thank you for choosing to stand for me. My ultimate prayer is that my life honors all of your sacrifices. Everything good about me is you. I honor you. And, I love you.

To my mentor and sister Karen Robinson, thank you for provoking me to greatness and seeing everything in me. I'll never forget the look you gave me while in Cambodia the first time. I love you.

To all who have taken time to pour into me and support me in some fashion – thank you, for your patience and love.

…after all, even late blossoms bloom.

CONTENTS

STRATEGY & METHODOLOGY..................................xi
DECLARE DICTIONARY..xiii
INTRODUCTION: DECLARE..xv

1: THOUGHTS...1

2: SELF..29

3: GRATITUDE...45

4: FEAR..59

5: EMOTION..73

6: HEALTH...85

7: RELATIONSHIPS..99

8: COMMUNICATION..113

9: BUSINESS | CAREER..125

10: MONEY | WEALTH..139

11: SPEAKING..153

12: SPIRITUALITY..165

CONCLUSION..179
ABOUT THE AUTHOR..181

*Change your thoughts and you will change your world.
Thoughts become things – choose the good ones.*

STRATEGY & METHODOLOGY

Things to know, to get the most out of this book.

This book is designed to be consumed over a 12-month period, providing practice and action to take, accordingly. However, many of you may finish before the intended time frame and that is fine as well. What is most important is to work with each declaration and note what obstacles, reactions, feelings, and thoughts you have about each one. Then, explore why each reaction came up and note whether it still supports you or if you have outgrown it and need to create a healthier relationship with that particular declaration.

The declarations presented within these pages represent common areas that my clients have found themselves stuck in, blocked by, hindered from, or having a poor relationship with. Interestingly enough, the same areas have provided the most healing, growth, and positive results for my clients after doing the necessary work to choose a more powerful perspective.

At the end of each section you will have an opportunity to create your own declaration and to reflect on your process. We love to hear your victories and what has shifted for you as you move through the various exercises. You can share those with us at info@GreatnessRealized.com.

DECLARE DICTIONARY

Here are a few terms to know and reference throughout this book.

affirmations |ˌafərˈmāSH(ə)ns| a series of words brought together to create life-altering shifts, providing points of access to shifts that catapult those who are hungry enough into the very visions and dreams they desire.

belief |bəˈlēf| a strong conviction, unshakeable, not bending or easily swayable. Taking no consideration to feeling, considering most feelings to be unreliable and fiction.

coach |kōCH| an individual professionally trained and skilled at holding space for others while reflecting greatness, uncovering potential potholes, shining light on blind spots, standing in the gap for what is unseen, and becoming a catalyst to propel others forward.

declaration |ˌdekləˈrāSH(ə)n| what is said or commanded with authority, grounded in belief.

digging |dig-iNG| to search, explore, think about, contemplate.

feelings |ˈfēliNGs| emotions that often lie to you and can be unreliable, even unstable. If left un-checked, they will leave you in ruins.

greatness |ˈgrātnəs| the quality of being great; brilliance, worth, power, merit, significance, excellence. The key component of our lives we are entrusted to excavate and mine out, that we might positively impact the lives of others.

mental fitness |ˈmen(t)l ˈfitnəs| the act of being mentally fit. Having a sound mind—not wishy-washy, swaying back and forth across polar opposite mindsets, or building a home in the valley of indecision.

messaging |ˈmesijiNG| phrases, thoughts, words, or loops, that impact us positively or negatively.

mind's eye |mind(s)ī| the vision you see for yourself when you close your eyes.

nugget |ˈnəgət| a key principle or component that can change the trajectory of your life.

support |səˈpôrt| to aid or assist.

shift |SHift| to move, pivot, change thinking, shift direction, or adjust outlook.

INTRODUCTION: DECLARE

Let's Celebrate!

First of all, thank you. Thank you for thinking enough of yourself to invest in yourself. I just want to celebrate you. I feel like a child on their birthday, bubbling over with adventure and anticipation for your moments to come. As I have lived, breathed, and walked out this book, I've experienced transformation in my life, and I know you will too.

This book will teach you the one thing that millions of people all across the globe are craving to learn: **how to win the war inside of your mind.** Everyone wants to learn how to win this mental battle—paying thousands, if not hundreds of thousands of dollars in resources or paying the high cost of hard knocks and brutal personal losses—as it affects every area of our lives. However, to win this war, you must become mentally fit. In reading this book, you will learn how to:

- ✓ uproot negativity
- ✓ remove broken thought patterns
- ✓ speak positively over your life and the lives of others
- ✓ grow in mental fitness
- ✓ find the root of horrible thinking
- ✓ take action in the direction of your goals

Because I'm constantly seeking growth, I continue to do this work as a daily practice and personal habit. And, I know you can do this too. I am well acquainted with the possibilities that await you. All the juicy, vibrant-color-filled possibilities specifically crafted just for you. They have your name on them. I'm reminded of the book by Dr. Seuss, *Oh, The Places You'll Go*, and am filled with the same hope for you. I hope this writing is simple, clear, and profound. I hope it propels you forward and catapults you into the future version of yourself — the one you envision in your mind.

If you've never had the privilege to experience a life coaching or mentoring relationship, I believe this book will be one of the greatest tools you will ever obtain. You are holding a year's worth of coaching, broken down into the compacted form of a book. Imagine working with a Coaching and Training Consultant who is formally trained as a transformative, high-impact and performance coach; who is committed to your goals, success, and results; who can see the gaps and blind spots you do not see and co-create the bridges and structures necessary for your success; who specializes in reinvention and power-packed strategies specifically designed to facilitate your breakthrough; and who catapults you into your next level and the juicy places you desire. That, my friend, is the gift and precious tool you are holding in your hand.

I remember vividly when I went through a year of my own professional life-coaching and training; I clearly recall the enormous and rapid shifts that took place in my life. That year was one of the greatest years of my life — it was messy, I cried, laughed, explored areas of me that I had locked away — I found joy, celebration, my essence, I made the largest single investment I'd ever made into my

INTRODUCTION: DECLARE

development at that time, and I showed up for me. I was all in. My life was shaken in the best way possible. I took lots of L's and Wins at the same time. It was the absolute best $25,000 investment I've ever made. It was one of the best gifts I've ever gifted myself, and one I would whole-heartedly gift to myself again.

Whether I had the money or not, I've never been scared to invest in myself (a.k.a. to bet on me). I do believe in formal education and paid for both my Bachelor's Degree in Organizational Communication (a hybrid business and communications degree) and MBA myself, in addition to investing in the accredited coaching and professional training program I mentioned above.

Why do I share this? I'm sharing for two reasons. The first being, I want you to know I have a history of investment that produces results, where I have done the work and invested the time. I am qualified to coach you, work with you, and hold space for you. Secondly, I believe things that really matter in your life have a cost, a price tag, an investment associated with them. Clients I support and work with invest thousands of dollars to work with me monthly, and this powerful gem is under $25, and affordable to anyone. This makes my heart smile. I'm so honored and proud to provide this point of access (access to facilitate the possibility to shift or change) and an outlet for you. I'm equally thrilled to hold space for you as you do the work and DECLARE words of reinvention over your life. I am honored and humbled that you are choosing to let me guide you through some potentially sticky and uncomfortable places in your life, trusting the process and your results to create a life you are fully present for, exactly the way you envision it, filled with all that is possible.

I can attest to the life-changing results this book produces and am excited to hear about what occurs in your life after you begin the process. I get chills when I think of the growth you will experience over the next year (or less), the doors that will begin to open for you, and the positive ground you'll take by leaps and bounds. All of this and more, simply because you now have a tangible access point to shift and create exactly what you want to see, by showing up for yourself and doing the work.

So, yes. You are holding a year's worth of coaching, compacted into book form that asks pivotal questions and provides you access points to shift the key areas in your life you've longed to changed. If you are already playing big, this book will elevate your game. If you desire to play big, then this book is for you and will usher you into the arena you desire. The secret sauce is intentionally designed to get you out of your own way—calling you to be present and accounted for in your own life. The invitation is for you to leave your mask behind, or even burn it. By design, the writing is intended to push you, to ask you uncomfortable questions, and to have you take action in the direction of your goals.

Hear me well: the best version of you is possible. The life you envision—the juicy vision you hold for yourself—is possible and can be realized, if and when you commit to confronting yourself and squashing your fear. Fear ruins more lives than anything else on our planet. Fear fosters false security, a love affair with mediocrity, and results in you never fulfilling your purpose or realizing your dreams. Fear will steal

INTRODUCTION: DECLARE

years of your life and rich experiences that were meant specifically for you. Decide to take action. When you feel fear, evict it from your thoughts and strip away any power it has over your life.

I know you have been victim to the glorious opinion of others who have told you…
Your dream is not possible…
Who you desire to be is not possible…
You're stupid…
You'll never make it…
You'll never make it without me…
No one will listen to you…
You'll never amount to anything…
…and the list goes on. The assault from others on your dreams, goals, and desires is real and the effects have rendered you paralyzed, if not lifeless.

Listen, those people, whoever they are, when taking the time to crush your vision, were speaking and acting from a place of fear themselves. Have they ever done what you desire to do? Are they who you desire to be? Stop allowing people with zero qualifications to dictate what is possible for you.

Stop allowing them to crush you.

Stop allowing them to place seeds of fear and doubt in you.

Stop being a victim.

Stop giving them permission to make you feel small.

Allow me to speak some life into you: You, my brave, dear heart, are a champion. You are an overcomer. You are more than what they say. You are more than what you see in the mirror. You are greater than where you are now. You are enough. You matter. You have a purpose. Your voice is needed, and you are necessary. You have exactly what you need right now to become, to do, to speak, and to have exactly what you say—DECLARE—you are. You were made for this moment and built to handle all that you've endured so far. This is your moment. This is your time.

In whatever way you are showing up in life right now, show up bigger. Play bigger. Allow your voice to speak louder. Get up. Dry your eyes. And put your feet on the ground. Stop listing the excuses and move, no—PUSH forward.

Because we are waiting on *you*.
Let's get started.

1

THOUGHTS

|thought -- (noun) an idea or opinion produced by thinking or occurring suddenly in the mind. The action or process of thinking.|

Have you ever seen a mustard seed? Mustard seeds are super small, smaller than a pea, or even a piece of quinoa. If not, quickly Google a mustard seed. *Isn't it stunning?* Were you expecting more? It looks so dull and small. Absolutely nothing about it says powerful, at first glance or even second glance. You could say it's unassuming.

Our thoughts are very much like a mustard seed. Small and unassuming, with one strong differentiator. Our thoughts are powerful! We have so many thoughts, too numerous to count, that flood our minds every minute of every second of every day. It's perplexing to think that something so small has so much power. Power over what we think, what we say, where we go, and over our hopes, dreams, and aspirations. What is accomplished, what is said, all the way down to how we live and govern our lives—it all stems from our thoughts. What happens when thoughts become activated? They become words—running around all over the place—that create, tear down, or simply breed stagnation and indifference. Our thoughts create the atmosphere and environment of our mind.

If one of the most powerful and underrated tools we have is our mind, then the next most powerful tool we have is our *words*. Our minds and our words—this two-pack combo is the epicenter that shapes what we see and experience, our beliefs, what we view as possible, and what we accomplish. Words have the power to create. They can frame, show vivid color, add texture, and so much more. Words can also cause us to bleed. Words can leave enormous damage, bruise the soul and even break the human spirit. Thoughts and words have created everything we see, touch, and experience. For example, they create our entertainment outlets and cause them to dance right in front of our eyes by way of a television series or movie.

Our thoughts allow us to share ideas and communicate. Our thoughts allow for connection and intimacy with others. Our thoughts can even cause sickness and pain when translated into words or if they are bottled up and buried for periods time. Our thoughts create environments and shift atmospheres, both positively and negatively. The daily news outlets are a perfect example of this, as many now opt out of what they feel is negative media. We are changing the way we consume content and even specify what we want to consume based on how we want to feel and based on the positive or negative atmospheres we want to allow access to us. Millennials, for example, have changed how the public consumes the news, as many find alternative outlets and consume media on demand.

What we think about consumes us. What we harbor affects our moods, opinions, and outlooks — even our health.

How is it that people are skeptical of affirmations or think that words have no power? Affirmations, in and of themselves, are powerless — unless the work has been done, or is being done, to till the soil of the mind so that when affirmations are planted, they grow in the rich soil of our belief. Affirmations are a series of words brought together to create life-altering shifts to those who are bold enough to grow. They provide points of access to those who are hungry enough, catapulting them into the life they envision — all because they began to DECLARE life over themselves and over their current situations.

No matter your beliefs, upbringing, socioeconomic standing, class, background, life experiences, education, what country you live in, your race, age, or ability, I do not believe it is an accident you are in possession of this book. I completely and firmly believe this is an access point — an opportunity, if you choose to accept it — that will alter your life in the most positive and amazing way possible. When thoughts are released from the rich soil of our mind as words — spoken, written, signed, or visualized — they immediately create an impact within your personal atmosphere. They immediately take shape. So now, before some of the more witty thinkers say, "I drive a Bugatti or a Range Rover" and get sorely disappointed when they walk outside to discover they still drive a Honda Coupe—know that it's not because this principle doesn't work. Think about when you are hungry. The message continues to circulate over and over in your mind (and stomach) until you may even say out loud, "I'm hungry." Now, your mind has engaged your speech, and you are on the hunt—not to be satisfied until the hunger alarm screaming through your body is sufficed. This is an example of the processes of immediacy where our thoughts engage our speech and impact our personal atmosphere.

Cars, homes, and other "larger ticket items" work within the same process. The messages we send are either positive or negative to our desire. At some point, we either choose to eat or choose not to eat. The choice is entirely ours to make. No matter what, the process is the same and the key to this process of manifesting the thought or desire you have (that will either work in your favor or against it) is consistency.

The power of your thoughts cannot be overstated or emphasized enough. Here are a few samples of perspectives from noteworthy individuals:

"As a man thinketh, so is he." **- James Allen**

"The happiness of your life depends on the quality of your thoughts." **- Marcus Aurelius**

"Everything you can imagine is real." **- Pablo Picasso**

"What we think determines what happens to us, so if we want to change our lives, we need to stretch our minds."
- Wayne Dyer

"Whether you think you can or think you can't. You're right." **- Henry Ford**

"You are today where your thoughts have brought you; you will be tomorrow where your thoughts take you."
- James Allen

"You must learn a new way to think before you can master a new way to be." **- Marianne Williamson**

"Nothing has any power over me other than that which I give it through my conscious thoughts." **- Tony Robbins**

"The world we have created is a product of our thinking; it cannot be changed without changing our thinking."
- Albert Einstein

"A man is but the product of his thoughts. What he thinks, he becomes." **- M. Gandhi**

"Man, alone, has the power to transform his thoughts into physical reality; man, alone, can dream and make his dreams come true." **- Napoleon Hill**

"Positive thinking will let you do everything better than negative thinking will." **- Zig Ziglar**

"You become what you believe." **- Oprah Winfrey**

"Nothing can stop the man with the right mental attitude from achieving his goal; nothing on earth can help the man with the wrong mental attitude." **- Thomas Jefferson**

"The ancestor to every action is a thought." **- Ralph Waldo Emerson**

All of these quotes can be summed up in one simple truth: our thoughts are so powerful that we can create and bring what we think about and believe into existence. Therefore, in order to properly manage the epicenters of our thoughts and our minds effectively, we must be and become mentally fit.

The foundation of life is thought. An idea. A concept. These foundational molecules percolate in our minds—the single richest soil for planting and getting a return that we will ever encounter. These molecules are not to be underestimated, as they are small but mighty and power-packed. These molecules are formed and shaped, coming out as words—spoken, written, signed, or visualized.

Here is where you get to be the hero in the story. This time, you get to rescue yourself and save the day. You get to be the one to provide your family with the life they dream of. You get to be the one to break barriers and do things that have yet to be done because you open your mouth with boldness and DECLARE life into your life.

All of this happens the moment you decide to shift your thoughts and DECLARE what you want to see. The introduction of this book highlighted learning points that you would dive into, explore, and take away actionable tools and steps to shift your life in pursuit of declaring what you see in your mind's eye and boldly taking steps to have your mouth and actions be in agreement and alignment. Since we are on the topic of thoughts and our minds, let's go ahead and unpack some necessary tools that are fundamental to your life and can dramatically shift you into the direction of the outcomes you strongly wish to create.

Uproot Negativity

Negativity is a mood-killer and a joy-stealer. We all know what it is like to be around negative people and how it feels to be in negative environments. Negativity is like walking into a toxic place. The toxic energy negativity brings with it always impacts all who come in contact with or interact with it.

Negativity impacts our perspective—how we view situations, whether or not we feel hopeful or optimistic, what we think of and even about others. Negativity is like that evil villain depicted in movies, cartoons, or other forms of entertainment. So, how do we navigate a negative space when the negative energy and space is within us, in our MINDS?

Negativity is definitely a barrier of entry to the most desired places, goals, dreams, and aspirations you may have. So, how can we even begin to reclaim the time, energy, damage, and resources impacted by our negative thoughts, self-talk, and patterns?

1. Become Aware. It's important to become aware of your thoughts. Just like kids have a babysitter, as not to be left unattended, it's important to begin to check-in on your thoughts and stop leaving them unattended. This first step is critical to the success of uprooting negativity in your life.

It is equally important to become aware of your thoughts without judging them. The only job or "to-do" here is to simply notice what you are thinking about. That's it.

2. Notice Themes. Now that you are aware, what are the key themes that you are seeing? What is the negativity centered around? What are the main comments you are saying to yourself about you? What are you noticing about the world around you and what sort of nasty negative comments are you making internally, in your mind? How are you tearing yourself down? Are you saying horrible comments? Are there choice, negative words you are using when you dialogue with yourself? Assessing these themes and finding commonalities will allow us to begin to dig a little deeper into the value you are getting by allowing this negativity and these types of conversations space in your life.

3. Ask. Let's go deeper. What would have you talking to yourself in this demeaning way? What would have you allowing this negative energy to continue to have room and board in your mind, impacting your thoughts and actions? Let's be clear: whether you know it or not, you are getting something from this little setup. Our task is to uncover what it is. Ask yourself the following two questions and pay attention to what bubbles up. (Don't talk yourself out of whatever shows up.) Once your eyes are closed and you have taken a deep breath, ask yourself this first question: *What am I getting from allowing negativity to be in my* *space in this way?* (If you feel like you don't know the answer, ask yourself, *If I knew why I am allowing this negativity to be in my space in this way, what would the reason be?*)

Nugget: For more layered areas such as pain or healing, implement gratitude and visualization. Gratitude to acknowledge the pain and visualization to practice relating to yourself as whole and complete, having received what is already available to you.

Practice: Now that you know the reason, even if you don't like the reason, you are going to practice noticing when negativity shows up for you and then replace those thoughts completely.

Examples:
I'm broke. → I'm so thankful I have everything I need right now. I await, with great expectation, and command the tangible manifestation of my desire to come now.
I'm lonely. → I have more love and connection than I thought possible. I intentionally open myself to connections that are in alignment with my highest good and ask for them to come now.
I hate my job. → My job is a great gift to me and I'm so blessed to have it. I open to and ask for the next level of my career to come now.

Do you see the difference between the negative thought and how you replace it? Immediately, you can see love and care for yourself and your desires just by how you replace the negative thoughts. This is what you do. These are the steps—rinse and repeat.

Note: You will get tired, annoyed, think this doesn't matter, feel like it should not take all this to get your thoughts and mental fitness together—but it does. Anything worth having has a price to pay. You have to be relentless in this area. You have to be unwavering. One more time for the people in the back who think I'm kidding—YOU GOTTA, AS IN, HAVE TO, BE RELENTLESS.

Whenever, I have a thought that does not align with my goals, what I desire, who I know myself to be, etc., I attack it immediately. I have NO room to fester negativity in my mind. I literally take hold of it, check it, let it know it is not welcome in my mind and kick it out—like for real, "Don't come back, I'm not going to be using my energy I on you. And if you do try me, and try to creep back in, I'm ready and will kick you out again." (These are the conversations I have with my thoughts! I am relentless and this works.)

While addictions have not been my struggle in life, I have had clients whose stories include addiction. People in my family and family tree, whom I share DNA with, have also struggled with various addictions. Because I know my personality, I know I have addictive traits, so I work to safeguard and strongly monitor what I allow in my life, what I experience, and the level of what I experience as a method of prevention. I know this method and these steps work because I've tried and tested them in my own life. These same steps even work for those who struggle with addiction.

One final note for those who struggle with addiction or have addictive personalities: Find the pain and confront it. Addiction, at the root, is typically triggered by pain and engaged as a method of coping, numbing, and anesthetizing the pain. Often, tools that are given or provided to those in pain or actively medicating their pain (through sex, shopping, drugs, abuse, drinking, work, food, etc.) address the symptom, not the root. Let's take a look at some examples.

Example: I'm fat. I'm overweight. I'm obese.
Symptom Fix: Social tools and resources recommend losing weight through diet and exercise.
Root Fix: What is the driver of overeating or excessive eating?

Example: Shopping or spending money when bills are not paid and current debt (credit card or other) needs to be paid.
Symptom Fix: Stop compulsive shopping. Sell clothes/items. Pawn items. Open another credit card.
Root Fix: What is driving the compulsive shopping while jeopardizing your basic needs and obligations? What about you is not enough? What are you compensating for?

The trouble with addiction is when the pain is loud enough, we will do anything to mask the pain — even sacrificing our own security. The trouble with fixing a symptom once the medication wears off is that we end up right back to where we started — with the pain. So, over time, we need our medicine to be stronger because we feel the pain more intensely. This can create a potentially vicious and detrimental cycle when we seek to fix the symptom (because it seems quicker and easier) instead of confronting the root of the pain. Find the pain, confront it by getting bold enough to get to the root, and BE RELENTLESS!

Remember, as you begin to uproot negativity and shift your thinking, you will not do this perfectly — but perfection is not the goal. The goal is practice! Practice without judgment and often. Practice noticing when you are carrying negative energy in your body, in your mind, and in your heart. Negativity isn't something to play with or entertain and can have severe effects on our physical health. Consider these tips while practicing:

1. Gratitude. When you choose to become present to everything you have as being a gift — from the air that fills your lungs, to the freedom of your body to move on its own, to the neurons firing in your brain, to the roof over your head, to having a place to sleep at night, to your friends, family, and loved ones, to the experiences of loss, joy, and happiness — you will begin to overflow. Gratitude and thanksgiving put us in the mindset of gratefulness and power. From this place, we will draw more good to ourselves and our mindsets will change because we are so thankful. Your gratitude can become so intense that you are able to overflow onto others, all of the time.

2. Self-Talk. Listen, sometimes you have to interrupt your own self-talk (the conversation going on in your mind) or it can get out of control. Disrupting these conversations can look like you checking yourself by saying or thinking these things:

"Nope, we are not going down this road."

"Who are you talking to in that way?"

"You will be more loving and demonstrate more care to me."

"I will no longer allow you to think this about _____. Period."

"This is not up for discussion."

"I am more than capable of achieving that goal, and this sort of talk will not be allowed."

"You will get up, you will get out of bed, and you will be amazing today."

"You will no longer hide or seclude yourself from the world any longer. You carry an amazing treasure and have value that the people around you absolutely need."

Can you see this pattern? Imagine, you have a best friend (if you don't have a best friend then imagine your momma), and someone is talking crap about your best friend. Someone is totally dogging them in front of you. While some of you will feel like fighting, others of you will no doubt check whoever is talking crap and set them straight! *Am I right? Why?* Because you don't play that game. Do you wish someone would come try you? Test you, even? You stay ready. All this energy you feel about your BFF (or your momma) now needs to be directed toward yourself! Apply that same energy to your own self-talk and even the negative environments you may find yourself in.

My dear, you are way too valuable, necessary, and important not to stick up for yourself. Listen, if I were around you, I'd for sure be sticking up for you and interrupting and disrupting your whole negative self-talk situation.

BONUS! While we are here, this same principle applies to accountability and holding yourself accountable for the goals YOU have and what YOU say YOU want to accomplish. Powerful Disruptors for accountability that you can ask/check yourself with include:

> *Is what I am doing now moving me closer to my goals or pushing me further away?*
>
> *Is this choice in alignment with what I want for my life?*
>
> *Is this action consistent with my revenue goal?*
>
> *Am I showing up consistently?*
>
> *Did I show up (in a visible manner) for myself and my goals today?*
>
> *What percentage did I show up/play at today?*
>
> *What are my top three items to accomplish today?*
>
> *What is the one thing I can focus on that will generate the most results?*

Who are the top 5 people I am surrounding myself with? (**Tip:** This can be a virtual goal. While you should take note of who is in your immediate circle, if your circle does not look like where you are going and where you want to be, find those who fit the description. We live in a digital age and this can be done easily with social media.)

Am I working efficiently?

Am I working on my written plan?
(Mental plans ALWAYS change—write it down!)

Am I taking in information, experiences, and visual imagery that is building me up?

What am I feeding on?

Are the goals I'm creating measurable?

Are my goals date and time stamped?

Do I set a time limit on the work I do to maximize my results or am I wasting my time by allowing infinite hours for completion?

These questions are power disruptors for accountability and literally the tip of the iceberg to getting you focused, engaged, and on track.

3. Powerful Questions: It's so important to check yourself. You are with yourself 24-7, 365. So, if

you don't like who you are, it will be obvious in how you deal with yourself. Your rewards, your celebration, the way you deal with tough times, and what you choose to medicate yourself with (sex, shopping, drugs, abuse, drinking, work, food, etc.). Because you are with yourself always, powerful questions serve as good disruptors to our typical thoughts. Here are some examples:
What would this answer be if I did know the answer?

What would my life look like if I were not afraid?

What would my life look like if I chose to move powerfully forward?

What choice would I make if I evicted fear?

How can I best love myself?

What would serve me most in this moment?

What would it be like to have both options?

How would it feel to create a more powerful conversation that served my purpose or goal?

What is my purpose?

What might I choose if I trusted that the money was already handled?

How might I express my gift and purpose more fully?

What would it look like if I showed up in my life, fully present and accounted for at 100%?

How would my life be different if I chose to play/engage/show up at 100% in every area of my life?

What shifts and breakthroughs could I create if I chose to be consistent?

What would my life look like if I wrote down my vision and created small, manageable steps to achieve what I see/desire?

Powerful questions, by nature, are designed to move and propel you forward.

Nugget: Typically, "why" is not a powerful question. By nature, "why" invites us to explore the current situation and dive deeper in. "Why," by nature, is explorative. Often, as we explore, it can become easy to get caught up in our mess, our reasons, and our broken thought processes (we call this a "construct" in coaching). Ultimately, we can all give, find, and muster excuses for our current situations, states, and positions in life. However, if we are to move powerfully forward, realizing and obtaining exactly what we see to be possible for our lives, we have zero time to lose and give to excuse. Period. Powerful questions catapult us into the juicy places we desire to be a part of and dwell in the most.

Broken Tapes

It's important to remove broken thought patterns that are no longer serving you—working toward your good. Often, these are messages that were ingrained in us as children that formed and shaped the structures of how we view and interact with both internal and external stimulants. Broken tapes (thoughts or thought patterns that loop in our mind) differ slightly from negative messaging because these types of messaging and patterns could have started as a positive or negative.

For example, growing up, privacy was a big message that was consistently drilled into my brothers and I. "Keep your mouth shut" and "don't talk about what goes on in our house" and "don't let people pump you for information" were all significant messages we heard that were seemingly harmless. These were just rules my mom had for whatever her reasons were and we just followed because she was our mom. Whenever we'd go somewhere, she'd take the opportunity to refresh our memories and set clear expectations for our behavior.

But here's where messages like this start to detour. Growing up, I didn't say much. Meaning, you could ask me a question and I'd answer it, but I was not sharing any more than what you needed to know. Subconsciously, I had been groomed to keep my mouth shut. I noticed, even yesterday, how this is still playing out in my life. I didn't know why I responded the way I did, but I know now.

One day, my mom came to pick me up from school, like she did every day. My mom is the bubbliest personality you will ever meet, so when I got in the car, she was super excited to see me. She did the "mom thing" by giving me a big hug and kiss and then asked me how my day was. I didn't answer her right away and by the time I did, I muddled the infamous, "Fine." I was only in the third grade and I was shutting down.

As the years passed, people began trusting me with their secrets, because I didn't share anything. I was a vault, a black hole. This should have been awesome, *right?* People were trusting me! But high school was hell on earth for me and I'm pretty sure that's when my mother earned her sainthood. In this stage of my life, I was closed off and isolated, dealing with really difficult situations, trying to navigate and process all that I was seeing, hearing, and being trusted with. The problem was, I didn't trust anyone, and was not ready to talk or share anything I was faced with and being exposed to.

I'm pretty sure my mom and I fought almost every day for four years. (I mentioned that she is a saint, *right?*) During those years, I was angry, scared, unsure, isolated, and mostly confused by the way others created, established, processed and asserted their world views — world views I thought to be stale, narrow-minded, shallow, and damaging to those who interacted with such people.

My brothers also faced their own battles with isolation, poor decision making, shame, and pride when feeling they should reach out and get support. So, they choose to keep their mouths shut and process their situations silently, with the only tools that were on their tool belt at the time.

As young adults, without our knowing, we came face-to-face with a construct called "privacy" that was created and introduced to us as children, with the absolute best intention. However, over time, this positive messaging, that was intended for our good (not to shame or hide situations that were harmful or detrimental to our well-being as children), began to no longer serve us. This faulty mindset began to break down and we each began to have our own significant run-in's with so-called "privacy." It was not until a significant event in my life occurred, and through watching my brothers experience significant events in their own lives, that the messages we received about privacy had absolutely expired and out-lasted their purpose and intent. Because of the challenges and obstacles we faced, it was critical that my brothers and I removed or replaced these broken tapes of faulty messaging.

I share this story progression with you as a point of access for you to look over your own life to see what core messaging is present, that may no longer be effective for your life. These tapes have to be monitored, as they simply loop in our minds. Stopping, removing, or replacing these tapes and their negative messaging is key to our freedom and our start to reinventing relationships and healthy patterns in life.

Mental Fitness

Mental fitness impacts every area of our lives and is the state of being mentally fit. Mental fitness is all about having a sound mind, being mentally sound — not wishy-washy, swaying back and forth across polar opposite mindsets, or building a home in the valley of indecision. Just like you work out to achieve a state of being physically fit, your mental fitness is the practice of exercising your mind in order to produce your desired results in other areas and aspects of your life. Our level of mental fitness is directly proportional to our success. It is foundational to how we grow and develop. It is fundamental to our thoughts, how we process and apply information, how we process our emotions and feelings, and how we cope and apply coping strategies.

Abundance is found at the intersection of your thoughts and beliefs.

Just like hitting the gym or working out with a personal trainer to get fit, mental fitness is the same. You have to exercise your mind in the same way you'd exercise your body—with strength and conditioning, diet, exercise, stretching, and weights to strengthen, tone and grow your level of cognitive health.

How do you know if you are mentally fit? A few indicators of mental fitness may include having self-discipline, resilience, foresight, flexibility, adaptability, patience, decisiveness, or emotional stability. If you don't see these attributes in your life right now—don't worry, just keep reading and we'll get there together.

Action Now
Practice taking action in your thoughts, now. Action is powerful. Action in the moment is king. It leaves no room for fear or for perfection.

THOUGHTS
DECLARATIONS

DECLARE: I can control what I think about.

What is easy for you to believe about this statement?

What makes it hard or difficult?

Where have you heard this?

List all messaging you have encountered around this.

Are you ready to shift?

Breakthrough Question: Are you willing to let go of any negative messaging around this so you can become the fullest, best version of you? Why am I whole?

Breakthrough Action:

DECLARE: My thoughts are subject to me.

What is easy for you to believe about this statement?

What makes it hard or difficult?

Where have you heard this?

List all messaging you have encountered around this.

Are you ready to shift?

Breakthrough Question: Are you willing to let go of any negative messaging around this so you can become the fullest, best version of you? Why am I whole?

Breakthrough Action:

DECLARE: Negative thought patterns are no longer welcome in my mind.

What is easy for you to believe about this statement?

What makes it hard or difficult?

Where have you heard this?

List all messaging you have encountered around this.

Are you ready to shift?

Breakthrough Question: Are you willing to let go of any negative messaging around this so you can become the fullest, best version of you? Why am I whole?

Breakthrough Action:

DECLARE: I can create what I visualize.

What is easy for you to believe about this statement?

What makes it hard or difficult?

Where have you heard this?

List all messaging you have encountered around this.

Are you ready to shift?

Breakthrough Question: Are you willing to let go of any negative messaging around this so you can become the fullest, best version of you? Why am I whole?

Breakthrough Action:

DECLARE: _____

What is easy for you to believe about this statement?

What makes it hard or difficult?

Where have you heard this?

List all messaging you have encountered around this.

Are you ready to shift?

Breakthrough Question: Are you willing to let go of any negative messaging around this so you can become the fullest, best version of you? Why am I whole?

Breakthrough Action:

Time to Check-In.

You did it! You are working those mental fitness muscles out and will be seeing positive results very soon. Shifting your perspective and digging into why things occur the way they occur for you is challenging—especially when our mental muscles are not accustomed to working out this way.

However, you're doing great!

In the space below, I want you to tell me what you would like to be acknowledged for.

To share, send what you just wrote to our email info@GreatnessRealized.com with the word "Acknowledgement" as the subject line.

2

SELF

|self — (noun) a person's essential being that distinguishes them from others, especially considered as the objects of introspection or reflexive action. Oneself in particular.|

The relationship you have with yourself sets the stage, tone, and creates the atmospheric-interaction for all you come in contact with. We are with ourselves more than we are with anyone else. If we need to talk, ring someone and can't get them — we are left by ourselves. If no one can hang out, we are left alone with ourselves.

This interpersonal relationship is critical and foundational to every other interaction and relationship we build. How we relate to who we are, what we think about ourselves, and our interpersonal self-interaction is very telling because it is the foundation we create, build, and stack other relationships upon. Relationships, external of us, are extensions of us. And we are the sole connective thread between our relationship with our interpersonal self and our external relationships.

In our societal messaging, there seems to be a context of perfection that has a message and a journey you can explore and adopt. This context is so damaging to self because it brings with it so many other contexts like, "enough," "worth," "acceptance," and "visibility," to name a few. Like crazed shoppers on a store sale day, we sort through these contexts trying each on in the fitting room of life to see if it fits. We are so preoccupied exploring this context of perfection wondering, *Am I enough? Am I worth it? Am I worthy? Am I accepted? Do people see me? Am I visible? Do I matter?*

Pause.

Are you *freaking* kidding? These are the questions we spend a good portion of our lives contemplating? This distorted context called perfection, that comes amazingly packaged as a treasure? It's a freaking rabbit hole that goes on forever and ever, literally robbing us blind of our time, experiences, relationships, opportunities, resources, and our very essence — all because of one big distraction that keeps us from the real goldmine of this interpersonal relationship with ourselves called *process*.

That's it!

Think about it. Our one job, our greatest gift and highest honor is the fact that we simply get to BE. We were given a gift called BE.

If this is our greatest gift, honor, and one job — then why is everything in our society (and the vast majority of what is pulling at you now) focused on separating you from this gift and opportunity? There is so much messaging pulling at you and ripping apart the seams of what holds you together that you can't recognize the goldmine of the process. The goldmine of *be*.

In this context called *process*, where the goldmine of *be* is located, you are no longer struggling with your worth—rather, you know your worth and explore how to best shift your worth from the interpersonal relationship with self to the external relationships you've created to serve and honor the best and highest form of your "be."

See, this context of process transcends beyond ourselves. In this space, we are like caterpillars becoming butterflies. We honor ourselves where we are and who we know to ourselves to be. In this space, we do not wonder if we are enough. We accept the knowledge that we are enough and shift it to our external side to create something that honors our highest self in the space of *be*. In this space, we do not wonder if we are accepted, because we function in the knowledge that we are accepted, thus shifting the interpersonal to the external, honoring our highest expression of *be*. In this space we do not wonder if we are seen; rather, we know we are seen and visible, so we move with fluidity from the interpersonal to the external, creating and honoring that which is our highest self in the space of *be*. In this space, we do not wonder if we matter, because we know we do, and function with the knowledge that we do matter. We created matter from our matter, and from that matter create what really matters, and move this knowledge from our interpersonal relationship to our externals, honoring our highest self in the space of *be*.

Does this sound narcissistic or bold to you? If we are but mirrors and reflections, how can honoring our highest self be narcissistic if we are only honoring the reflection of the image in which we were made? But, *bold?* Absolutely. Bold, because many of us are somewhere down the rabbit hole, looking for the light at the end of the tunnel, and frustrated because we cannot see.

We are multi-dimensional beings. Because we are multi-dimensional, we can shift our thoughts. We can adopt new ways of thinking, processing, and the messages we send, receive, and store. We can learn and unlearn.

We can create something tangible from nothing more than a thought.

If we are tired of being in the never-ending-tunnel, we can think a new thought and transition our lives to a new place—the place we desire, that we can touch and feel with our hands.

This is why your thoughts are so important. Your mind is a treasure chest waiting for you to move what's inside—the interpersonal to the external—into a tangible form.

You are the "who," "what," "when," "where," "why," and "how" you have been waiting for.

Our thoughts are important because the interpersonal relationship with self— ourselves—is completely constructed and contingent upon our thoughts. The conversation between the interpersonal relationship with self and your thoughts determines which context you choose: perfection or process.

Re-read that last sentence.

This is so important to understand. The choice between the context of perfection or process is emphatically important because it determines how much time, resources, energy, relationships, years, money, opportunities you lose, forfeit, give up, or automatically move to the liabilities side of the equation. The conversation you have in your mind determines your choices and outlook on life. Period. Additionally, the erosion of your essence—the beautiful being you are—is costly as well.

There is a cost to the context of perfection. For clarification, it is not to say lessons are not learned in and from this context. The crux is this: if you, where you are, could, in fact, be sat down and given the details of every situation you will experience before you experience it, your conversation would change. Your options would change. If you are driving and your friend informs you that there is a huge pothole ahead and you swerve to miss it because they gave you a forewarning, you would consider that to be valuable information because they provided access for you to make a different choice than you would have had you not known. That choice may have saved you potential time, resources, energy, stress, money, etc. if you would have blown a tire or made other damages to your car. If you had not followed your friend's advice and chose to do something else, you would still learn to not hit potholes—but it would be a much more painful (and expensive) lesson.

In the same way, understanding *self* is key to many of the issues you are exploring now. Because this interpersonal relationship is so important, we have a great opportunity to move the dial and take massive ground though shifting or enhancing this relationship.

Let's take a moment to gain some outside perspectives on *self* and its importance. Take a look:

"If you have no confidence in self, you are twice defeated in the race of life." **- Marcus Garvey**

"Loneliness is the poverty of self; solitude is the richness of self." **- May Sarton**

"Every human has four endowments: self-awareness, conscience, independent will, and creative imagination. These give us the ultimate human freedom… The power to choose, to respond, to change." **- Steven Covey**

"This above all; to thine own self be true."
- William Shakespeare

"Trust yourself. Create the kind of self that you will be happy to live with all your life. Make the most of yourself by fanning the tiny, inner sparks of possibility into flames of achievement." **- Golda Meir**

"Loving oneself isn't hard when you understand who and what 'yourself' is. It has nothing to do with the shape of your face, the size of your eyes, the length of your hair or the quality of your clothes. It's so beyond all of those things and it's what gives life to everything about you. Your own self is such a treasure." **- Phylicia Rashad**

"Self-love has very little to do with how you feel about your outer self. It's about accepting all of yourself."
- Tyra Banks

"The ego is only an illusion, but a very influential one. Letting the ego-illusion become your identity can prevent you from knowing your true self. Ego, the false idea of believing that you are what you have or what you do, is a backwards way of assessing and living life." **- Wayne Dyer**

"Inner beauty should be the most important part of improving one's self." **- Priscilla Presley**

"There is nothing noble in being superior to your fellow men. True nobility lies in being superior to your former self." **- Ernest Hemingway**

"If you do not conquer self, you will be conquered by self." **- Napoleon Hill**

"Remember who you always were, where you came from, who your parents were, how they raised you. That authentic self is going to follow you all through life. Make sure that it's solid, so it's something you can hold on to and be proud of for the rest of your life." **- Michelle Obama**

"Sometimes you've got to let everything go — purge yourself. If you are unhappy with anything... what is bringing you down, get rid of it. Because You'll find that when you're free, your true creativity, your true self comes out." **- Larry Chang**

"Friendship with oneself is all important because without it one cannot be friends with anyone else in the world." **- Eleanor Roosevelt**

"The most painful thing is losing yourself in the process of loving someone too much and forgetting that you are special too." **- Ernest Hemingway**

"Yesterday I was clever, so I wanted to change the world. Today I am wise, so I am changing myself." **- Rumi**

"Many a book is like a key to unknown chambers within the castle of one's own self." **- Franz Kafka**

"We are taught you must blame your father, your sisters, your brothers, the school, the teachers—but never blame yourself. It's never your fault. But it's always your fault because if you wanted to change, you're the one who has got to change." **- Katherine Hepburn**

"If you cannot find peace within yourself, you will never find it anywhere else." **- Marvin Gaye**

"Don't be surprised by your greatness. Be surprised that no one expected it." **- Rebecca Maizel**

At the beginning of this chapter, we noted that we are with ourselves more than any other person. Because of this, we tend to see clearly the things about our character that we want to strengthen, habits we desire to break, new structures, new outlooks, and new attitudes we would like to operate from. Sometimes we get frustrated with ourselves--it can even feel like an internal war of sorts—because what we know to do, we don't; and instead, we do the opposite.

Why is that? We know where we align on the spectrum of "right" and "wrong" --so why are we at such odds with ourselves? This battle, and others like it, are shifted, won, repositioned, and work in our favor because we can choose new thoughts that support positive growth, development, and a healthy interpersonal relationship with ourselves.

Our thoughts and the interpersonal relationship we have with *self*, are critical to maintaining your mental fitness. If you allow your thoughts to run around like a little naked man, or if you allow your interpersonal relationship with *self* to be somewhere down the rabbit hole, you will remain mentally out-of-shape—even mentally obese. You will remain unhealthy and ill-equipped to handle simple processing aspects as it relates to the interpersonal relationship with *self* because you have refused to develop your muscles and create the stamina and environment you need to flourish.

Refusal doesn't always come in the form of an all-out temper tantrum. It doesn't always show up in the form of a rebellious no. Refusal can be quiet or silent as well. An inability or no response can be a refusal. It is simply an extremely quiet no. Keep this in mind as you process your interpersonal relationship with *self*. This will help you identify what context you are in and what is keeping you stuck or allowing you to shift as you desire.

The most important asset we have is our *self*. Therefore, we must be whole. Believe that everything works for your good. Be willing to stop hiding, take responsibility in your life and give yourself permission to do whatever you've been holding yourself back from doing, especially if it allows your highest self to shine.

Action Now

Practice taking action in the relationship you have with yourself, now. Action is powerful. Action in the moment is king. It leaves no room for fear or for perfection.

SELF
DECLARATIONS

DECLARE: I am whole.

What is easy for you to believe about this statement?

What makes it hard or difficult?

Where have you heard this?

List all messaging you have encountered around this.

Are you ready to shift?

Breakthrough Question: Are you willing to let go of any negative messaging around this so you can become the fullest, best version of you? Why am I whole?

Breakthrough Action:

DECLARE: All things work for my good.

What is true for you in regard to this declaration?

What makes it hard or difficult?

Do you believe this?

List all messaging you have encountered around this.

Will you allow yourself to believe this?

Breakthrough Question: Are you willing to let go of any negative messaging around this so you can become the fullest, best version of you? Why do all things work for my good?

Breakthrough Action:

DECLARE: I choose to take responsibility for my life.

What is easy for you to believe about this statement?

What makes it hard or difficult?

Where have you heard this?

List all messaging you have encountered around this.

Are you ready to shift?

Breakthrough Question: Are you willing to let go of any negative messaging around this so you can become the fullest, best version of you? Why do I choose to take responsibility for my life?

Breakthrough Action:

DECLARE: I give myself permission.

What is easy for you to believe about this statement?

What makes it hard or difficult?

Where have you heard this?

List all messaging you have encountered around this.

Are you ready to shift?

Breakthrough Question:
Are you willing to let go of any negative messaging around this so you can become the fullest, best version of you? Why do I give myself permission?

Breakthrough Action:

DECLARE: _____

What is easy for you to believe about this statement?

What makes it hard or difficult?

Where have you heard this?

List all messaging you have encountered around this.

Are you ready to shift?

Breakthrough Question: Are you willing to let go of any negative messaging around this so you can become the fullest, best version of you?

Breakthrough Action: Practice noticing where you do not feel whole. Note thoughts that would have you feel less than whole. Practice countering those negative thoughts and replacing them with thoughts that are in alignment with being whole.

Time to Check-In.

You did it! You are working those mental fitness muscles out and will be seeing positive results very soon. Shifting your perspective and digging into why things occur the way they occur for you is challenging—especially when our mental muscles are not accustomed to working out this way.

However, you're doing great!

In the space below, I want you to tell me what you would like to be acknowledged for.

To share, send what you just wrote to our email info@GreatnessRealized.com with the word "Acknowledgement" as the subject line.

3

GRATITUDE

| **gratitude** — (noun) the quality of being thankful; readiness to show appreciation and to return kindness. |

Gratitude has played a huge role in my life and I want to offer a bit of a personal reflection here and share briefly. I do not believe that gratitude is a magical fix, nor do I believe it is powerless. Rather, gratitude is most essential to mental fitness, focus, and achievement.

    Gratitude is all about how you are positioned and how your communication channel or communication system is set up. To achieve a goal requires some level of intentionality, meaning you deciding to put in the work for your goal, come hell or high water. Period. Gratitude sets the stage for achievement. Gratitude creates an open door. Gratitude is a road map when you don't see a way.

    There have been times when I've been so beat down and mentally fatigued — almost in a depressive state — with tons of negative thoughts flooding my mind (not to mention, the negative and less-than-optimal environment surrounding me).

Without fail, each time I found myself in that state, gratitude would act as a life raft, being tossed overboard for me to grab hold of, as I began to reflect on what I had. My health, home, car, clothes, food, water, tires, no bills, safety, friendship—just to name a few. As I began to think of small things, more things would start to flood my mind. Gas for my car, money to purchase gas, money to eat, blankets, clean water, family, breath in my body, etc. These tiny things (that seemed really insignificant) were major in that, as each one that came, they began to grab hold of the negative thoughts in my mind and body slam them down, taking their power away.

Gratitude gave me access to shift my mindset while providing me an opportunity to create my future through my thoughts.

In this aspect, gratitude is very much like a pencil. Ready to sketch and create what I see through the door of being grateful and thankful. Think about that.

What would it be like for you if you embodied continual thankfulness?

What would your life be like if you were thankful in every moment of every day, whether those moments were "good" or "bad"?

There have been times I've needed doors to open the "right" connection and could not see how or where what I desired would come from. Tuning into my journey, where I've come from, who I am, my evolution as a person; all the goodies that are stuffed inside of me—all the care, compassion, love, big-heartedness, that equally share space with the questions, worry, doubt, fear, untrue stories and more—I get so full of gratitude and start to overflow.

Did you know that if you are empty and feel like you have nothing left to give or pour out, you can open the door of gratitude and fill yourself back to full and create an overflow from that space? The same is true if you feel brokenness or heartache. Gratitude will do the same for you.

Let's explore the impact of gratitude through the perspectives of others you may know:

"Feeling gratitude and not expressing it is like wrapping a present and not giving it." **- William Arthur Ward**

"As we express our gratitude, we must never forget that the highest appreciation is not to utter words, but to live by them." **- John F. Kennedy**

"Gratitude can transform common days into thanksgiving, turn routine jobs into joy, and change ordinary opportunities into blessings." **- William Arthur Ward**

"Gratitude is not only the greatest of virtues but the parent of all the others." **- Marcus Tulles Cicero**

"Gratitude is the healthiest of all human emotions. The more you express gratitude for what you have, the more likely you will have even more to express gratitude for."
- Zig Ziglar

"Cultivate the habit of being grateful for every good thing that comes to you, and to give thanks continuously. And because all things have contributed to your advancement, you should include all things in your gratitude."
- Ralph Waldo Emerson

"Piglet noticed that even though he had a very small heart, it could hold a rather large amount of gratitude."
- A.A. Milne, Winnie the Pooh

"Start each day with a positive thought and a grateful heart." **- Roy T. Bennett**

"Be thankful for everything that happens in your life; it's all an experience." **– Roy T. Bennett**

"Great things happen to those who don't stop believing, trying, learning, and being grateful." **– Roy T. Bennett**

"Always remember people who have helped you along the way, and don't forget to lift someone up."
- Roy T. Bennett

"Let gratitude be the pillow upon which you kneel to say your nightly prayer. And let faith be the bridge you build to overcome evil and welcome good." **- Maya Angelou**

"Those who have the ability to be grateful are the ones who have the ability to achieve greatness."
- Steve Maraboli

"Gratitude unlocks the fullness of life." **- Anonymous**

"Gratitude opens the door to the power, the wisdom, the creativity of the universe. You open the door through gratitude." **- Deepak Chopra**

"When gratitude becomes an essential foundation in our lives, miracles start to appear everywhere."
- Emmanuel Dagher

"It's not happiness that brings us gratitude. It's gratitude that brings us happiness." **– Anonymous**
"Living in a state of gratitude is the gateway to grace."
- Arianna Huffington

"Be thankful for what you have; you'll end up having more. If you concentrate on what you don't have, you will never, ever have enough." **- Oprah Winfrey**

"When you are grateful fear disappears and abundance appears." **- Tony Robbins**

    This very real and tangible point of access is a vehicle that will allow you to shift any circumstance and atmosphere. It is a sign that says you are ready and open to what you desire, what you are seeking, and what is for you. The practice of gratitude (meaning to incorporate gratitude into your lifestyle) is life-changing. You will be amazed when you begin to intentionally integrate gratitude as a lifestyle.

    Gratitude is like FedEx, USPS, or the Internet for mail. It is the channel or means of communication by which we send or receive. Gratitude can also be likened to a car oil. Sure, a car will run for a period of time without oil. But the quality of how it will run is a completely different story.

    Gratitude is the same way. You don't have to exercise gratitude, but your life might seem to be more difficult in comparison to someone who does exercise gratitude. Their life might appear easier, simply because they have utilized the lubricant of gratitude.

Does this ring a bell or sound familiar?

Have you ever been in a situation where you felt mad or sad? Chances are that we've all experienced these emotions before or have witnessed someone else's mad or sad states and I bet, in both cases, the ability to focus on something else was next to impossible because of how mad or sad you or they were feeling.

Let's take it one step further.

Have you ever felt a void or emptiness inside of yourself, but you didn't know why?

Or, perhaps, you knew why, but no matter how hard you tried, you could not find anything to fill the void?

Have you ever blamed someone else for something that was their fault, even if you played a small role in the issue?

Do you ever wait and wait, and wait and wait for the perfect time to pursue a dream or goal?

In this chapter, we looked inward through the lens of gratitude to flex and exercise our mental muscles. The most important asset you have is YOU. Therefore, you must be whole, knowing that everything works for your good.

Be willing to go all in for yourself and take ownership of your life. This is the only way you will begin to access that level you know exists for you.

Action Now

Practice taking action in your gratitude, now. Action is powerful. Action in the moment is king. It leaves no room for fear or for perfection.

GRATITUDE DECLARATIONS

DECLARE: My attitude is gratitude.

What is easy for you to believe about this statement?

What makes it hard or difficult?

Where have you heard this?

List all messaging you have encountered around this.

Are you ready to shift?

Breakthrough Question: Are you willing to let go of any negative messaging around this so you can become the fullest, best version of you? Why is my attitude that of gratitude?

Breakthrough Action:

DECLARE: I am filled with gratitude and thanksgiving.

What is easy for you to believe about this statement?

What makes it hard or difficult?

Where have you heard this?

List all messaging you have encountered around this.

Are you ready to shift?

Breakthrough Question: Are you willing to let go of any negative messaging around this so you can become the fullest, best version of you? Why am I filled with gratitude and thanksgiving?

Breakthrough Action:

DECLARE: I am thankful for the limitless, overflowing source of my abundance.

What is easy for you to believe about this statement?

What makes it hard or difficult?

Where have you heard this?

List all messaging you have encountered around this.

Are you ready to shift?

Breakthrough Question: Are you willing to let go of any negative messaging around this so you can become the fullest, best version of you? Why am I thankful for the limitless, overflowing source of abundance?

Breakthrough Action:

DECLARE: I am grateful for all of my abundance and for that on its way to me.

What is easy for you to believe about this statement?

What makes it hard or difficult?

Where have you heard this?

List all messaging you have encountered around this.

Are you ready to shift?

Breakthrough Question: Are you willing to let go of any negative messaging around this so you can become the fullest, best version of you? Why am I grateful for all my abundance and for that on its way for me?

Breakthrough Action:

DECLARE: _____

What is easy for you to believe about this statement?

What makes it hard or difficult?

Where have you heard this?

List all messaging you have encountered around this.

Are you ready to shift?

Breakthrough Question: Are you willing to let go of any negative messaging around this so you can become the fullest, best version of you?

Breakthrough Action:

Time to Check-In.

You did it! You are working those mental fitness muscles out and will be seeing positive results very soon. Shifting your perspective and digging into why things occur the way they occur for you is challenging—especially when our mental muscles are not accustomed to working out this way.

However, you're doing great!

In the space below, I want you to tell me what you would like to be acknowledged for.

To share, send what you just wrote to our email info@GreatnessRealized.com with the word "Acknowledgement" as the subject line.

4

FEAR

|fear — (noun) an unpleasant emotion caused by the belief that someone or something is dangerous, likely to cause pain, or a threat.|

How often have we let fear stop us or keep us from pursuing our goals or stepping out of our comfort zones? It is said, that more dreams are killed by fear than anything else. It is also said that everything we really want exists, just on the other side of our comfort zone.

There are many acronyms we've heard that we can associate and identify with fear. I believe fear was given to us as a tool, an informant, if you will, to act as a guide on our behalf so that when a new sensory is brought into our space, we are invited to notice whatever is new about our environment and operate with higher intention and awareness. However, most of us take fear to the next level and misuse it outside of its design.

When we give in to fear, we don't move forward, don't take action, are paralyzed, and crumble our hopes, dreams, and aspirations into the trash—all while shutting down our lives. Most often, we make horrible decisions from a place of fear. We were designed to have a sound mind and to be mentally fit. As mentally fit people, we are not unstable, nor do we give in to fear. Rather, we steamroll it over.

We completely abandon the intent of fear and shift its role of an informant guide to a tyrant that restricts us to limiting beliefs, borders, boundaries, careers, lifestyles, relationships, and anything else that will keep us small and not our full selves.

    Make no mistake, there are instances where fear is good—and even healthy. This healthy fear is not what we are referencing. When we experience fear from this healthy place, we know that our informant is operating in the capacity it was designed to. However, fear that paralyzes from moving forward with our lives or moving outside of our comfort zone or what is familiar to us, is not healthy.

    We've discussed that many people encounter this type of fear when beginning to move outside their comfort zones and positively take ground in their lives. When this occurs, they've usually locked their sights on a goal or marker far enough down the road that they can see, and not lose sight of. However, what happens when we lose sight of the goal ahead is that we start to focus on our insecurities, our inadequacies, and the barriers in our path.

    Fear is the single greatest adversary to a dream. Even before the dream can take its first full breath in your mind, fear is there to kill and abort the glimmer of hope of your dream. Have you ever noticed that when you start looking at your limitations, shortcomings, insecurities, etc. that fear is overwhelming present? Fear can be so thick that it overwhelms and clouds the senses. When we lose sight of the bigger picture, the end goal, the "why," or our reason for beginning in the first place—fear eats us alive.

Fear ruins more lives than anything else on our planet. Fear fosters false security, a soul-robbing love affair with the mediocre, resulting in you never fulfilling your purpose or realizing your dreams. Fear will steal years of your life and rich experiences that were meant specifically for you.

Nelson Mandela said it best, "Our deepest fear is that we are powerful beyond measure. It is our light, not our darkness that most frightens us." We fear that we are far more powerful and more capable than we will ever imagine or realize.

Let's gain some additional perspectives on fear:

"Avoiding danger is no safer in the long run than outright exposure. The fearful are caught as often as the bold."
- Helen Keller

"One of the greatest discoveries a man makes, one of his great surprises, is to find he can do what he was afraid he couldn't do." **- Henry Ford**

"I have learned over the years that when one's mind is made up, this diminishes fear; knowing what must be done does away with fear." **- Rosa Parks**

"Fears are nothing more than a state of mind."

- Napoleon Hill

"I learned that courage was not the absence of fear, but the triumph over it. The brave man is not he who does not feel afraid, but he who conquers that fear." **- Nelson Mandela**

"The eagle has no fear of adversity. We need to be like the eagle and have a fearless spirit of a conqueror."

- Joyce Meyer

"Action cures fear, inaction creates terror."

- Douglas Horton

"Do the thing you fear to do and keep on doing it… that is the quickest and surest way ever yet discovered to conquer fear." **– Dale Carnegie**

We often hear, "Feel the fear and do it anyway." While this common saying is somewhat helpful, it can be really damaging if we are not careful. For instance, if you are already afraid of doing something (i.e. speaking, writing a book, taking a job, asking her/him out on a date, moving across the country or globe, or leaving your job for a new career), feeling the fear and doing it anyway is not the most effective mantra. Often, when trying to "feel the fear and do it anyway," you are stuck and stagnant, taking unfavorable action as it relates to your desire or dream.

I'd like to submit to you another way of thinking. Beyond the instinct of fear, used to protect us and serve us, fear should in no way be our master. When fear takes the role of controlling us, mastering over us, dictating what we can and can't accomplish, holding us back from our dreams and goals, standing in the way of what it is we really want—then we have to level up our approach. This type of fear has no place in your life. You were never meant to be roommates with this type of fear or to allow it residence in your heart, mind, or soul. This is the type of fear you do not negotiate with. This type of fear you boot out of your life, completely.

Take your power back! From this day forward, you will no longer be run by fear. Serve it an eviction notice from your life because you are powerful, filled with love, and have a sound mind. However, this type of fear makes you think otherwise. It makes you doubt your choices and capabilities. You may know what you are capable of in your heart, but when you move to take action in alignment with what you know to be true or see, fear will have you doubting and questioning all of your choices. This creates double-mindedness; and, if you are unstable in your thoughts and decisions, you'll get rocked by life because you will go back and forth constantly in your mind and actions.

The battlefield of fear is in your mind, and it is here that you can take ground and win! This is where you practice discipline. This is where your life begins to take shape, becoming all that you've imagined it to be. This is where the magic happens. This is the fight of your life. And, just in case you didn't know or thought otherwise, allow me a moment to welcome you to the fight for your life, hopes, and dreams.

This is where you fight for everything you love, want, desire, dream for, or see in your future. This, right here, is the ground of decision. And just in case you've been paying attention to the score or keeping track in your mind of how this fight with fear is going—who's winning or who's losing—if you think you are behind or losing this battle, let me quickly reframe this. Up until now, you've been fighting the wrong way. You've been showing up to battle with the wrong strategy and weapon.

So, while it's looked one way, while you think the score is not in your favor, I'm here to let you know that the fear in your life is a liar. Fear has been misinforming you of your power, authority, your right to rule over it, and leading you to believe that you are not the very embodiment of love completely expressed. Fear plays mental games with you causing you to feel unsure, unstable, and to doubt your skills and abilities. Listen, if you can't do it in this moment, I will do it for you. I will evict fear and every lie it's formed in your life and mind right now. It can no longer stay. It does not have the power and authority to stay because you were created to have dominion over it.

From this day forward, you will live unleashed, walking in the dreams, goals, and purpose you see for your life. You will walk in power and love, fully and completely expressed.

If you're struggling with fear, go back and revisit Chapter 1: *Thoughts* and reference "Uprooting Negativity" for the tangible steps to walk yourself through the process of uprooting fear.

Uprooting fear is just like pulling weeds from a garden. Fear has to be pulled up and tossed out. Now, it's up to you to do the work to keep fear from taking the ground it has no business occupying.

Action Now

Practice taking action against fear, now. Action is powerful. Action in the moment is king. It leaves no room for fear or for perfection.

FEAR DECLARATIONS

DECLARE: Love is bigger than my greatest fear.

What is easy for you to believe about this statement?

What makes it hard or difficult?

Where have you heard this?

List all messaging you have encountered around this.

Are you ready to shift?

Breakthrough Question: Are you willing to let go of any negative messaging around this so you can become the fullest, best version of you? Why is love bigger than my greatest fear?

Breakthrough Action:

DECLARE: I release the shame that comes with fear, enticing me to be less than.

What is easy for you to believe about this statement?

What makes it hard or difficult?

Where have you heard this?

List all messaging you have encountered around this.

Are you ready to shift?

Breakthrough Question: Are you willing to let go of any negative messaging around this so you can become the fullest, best version of you? Why do I release the shame that comes with fear, enticing me to be less than I am?

Breakthrough Action: Practice noticing where you do not feel whole. Note thoughts that would have you feel less than whole. Practice countering those thoughts and replacing them with thoughts in alignment with being whole.

DECLARE: I release fear from every place in my life, embracing the fullness of love and its strength.

What is easy for you to believe about this statement?

What makes it hard or difficult?

Where have you heard this?

List all messaging you have encountered around this.

Are you ready to shift?

Breakthrough Question: Why do I release fear from every place in my life, embracing the fullness of love and its strength?

Breakthrough Action: Practice noticing where you do not feel whole. Note thoughts that would have you feel less than whole. Practice countering those thoughts and replacing them with thoughts in alignment with being whole.

DECLARE: I choose to combat fear through the light of transparency, being vulnerable, and through the power of love.

What is easy for you to believe about this statement?

What makes it hard or difficult?

Where have you heard this?

List all messaging you have encountered around this.

Are you ready to shift?

Breakthrough Question: Why do I choose to combat fear through the light of transparency, being vulnerable, and through the power of love?

Breakthrough Action:

DECLARE: _____

What is easy for you to believe about this statement?

What makes it hard or difficult?

Where have you heard this?

List all messaging you have encountered around this.

Are you ready to shift?

Breakthrough Question: Are you willing to let go of any negative messaging around this so you can become the fullest, best version of you?

Breakthrough Action: Practice noticing where you do not feel whole. Note thoughts that would have you feel less than whole. Practice countering those thoughts and replacing them with thoughts in alignment with being whole.

Time to Check-In.

You did it! You are working those mental fitness muscles out and will be seeing positive results very soon. Shifting your perspective and digging into why things occur the way they occur for you is challenging—especially when our mental muscles are not accustomed to working out this way.

However, you're doing great!

In the space below, I want you to tell me what you would like to be acknowledged for.

To share, send what you just wrote to our email info@GreatnessRealized.com with the word "Acknowledgement" as the subject line.

5

EMOTION

| **emotion** — (noun) a natural instinctive state of mind deriving from one's circumstances, mood, or relationships with others. |

Emotions are simple, yet complex. They are the visual expression of our words. Imagine watching a movie that had no images or actors, only words. Add emotions—and boom—the lights are on and there is a picture. Emotions color in our lives in vibrant ways across the spectrum. But as wonderful as emotions are, when left unchecked, they can wreck your life and bring you to ruin. We've all seen it. That one extremely angry person that no one wants to be around. Or maybe the person with an addiction issue (to food, sex, drugs, alcohol, porn, shopping, etc.) because they are trying to cover a giant void in their lives.

Emotions are to people what a steering wheel is to a car, or what a rudder is to a boat. Emotions guide us. Now, whether or not we allow our emotions to dictate which roads we go down based on how we feel is a completely different issue altogether. Managing emotions and having a good handle on them really makes a difference in the opportunities and doors that open in our favor and plays a huge role in not rushing various seasons of our lives. The same is true when you mishandle seasons of your life—you can move too fast and rush it or move too slow and hold it up, causing a traffic jam on your flow highway.

We've all seen the artwork of children. When they take their time, they generally are able to produce something that looks great for their skill level. However, when they rush or are preoccupied or distracted by something else, their artwork looks like a tornado. Similarly, emotions are like little children. When left unchecked, they become spoiled, bratty, undisciplined and unpleasant to be around.

At the beginning, middle, and end of the day, it is important to remember that you are not your emotions and they do not rule or control you.

If you find yourself out of balance with your emotions, it's important to start taking small steps. You'll have to enforce discipline within yourself, but just start small, and then begin to expand what you require of your emotions. Remember, there is no shame in the process; it's just simple work to be done, like tidying a house. Perhaps you need to slow down or not indulge yourself in certain areas. Maybe you need to implement taking immediate action if you are scared or feel unprepared. Maybe you need practice at failing and getting back up. Pain is an unavoidable life guide full of lessons—and something we should not run from.

Emotions can often misinform and mislead us to act. Think about how many emotions you've felt this week. Who have you been upset with? How long did it last? What made you happy and what was the cause of your happiness? How long did it last before your next emotion was felt? When you were by yourself, what did you feel? When your friend didn't answer your call or text right away, what story did you create in your mind? How did your emotions play a role in supporting or talking you out of the story you were creating about the other person?

Still can't see it? Who did you have to work with this week at your job that you don't like? What did the customer or client say to you that rubbed you the wrong way? Did your boss come in? Did they give someone else more attention than you? Have you pinpointed your emotions yet? Do you see how they inform you about your personal world and all that is within it?

Some of you are a bit more extreme. What makes you go from 0-60 on the anger scale in less than two seconds? What makes you snap? What makes you hostile? What makes you angry? What is missing for you? What are you not able to properly communicate and articulate? What has you hurting the ones you love with your words or actions? What are you afraid of? What has you thinking your behavior is okay and appropriate? Who did you see model this behavior and these dramatic swings? Do you want to continue to live this way? Do you want to continue to have a front row seat to the damage you and your emotions are creating in the lives of others? Are you ready to make a more powerful choice? If so, every time you begin to feel the rage, sadness, or polarizing emotion, begin to practice how you want to handle that moment. It's okay if it's not perfect, our goal is to practice. The more you practice, the better you'll get and the more you'll begin to see yourself handling your emotional state in alignment with your desires. But don't just take it from me. Here are a few more perspectives on emotions that you can glean from:

"Negative emotions like loneliness, envy, and guilt have an important role to play in a happy life; they're big, flashing signs that something needs to change."
- Gretchen Rubin

"The sign of an intelligent people is their ability to control their emotions by the application of reason."
- Marya Mannes

"If your emotional abilities aren't in hand, if you don't have self-awareness, if you are not able to manage your distressing emotions, if you can't have empathy and have effective relationships, then no matter how smart you are, you are not going to get very far." **- Daniel Goleman**

"I don't want to be at the mercy of my emotions. I want to use them, to enjoy them, and to dominate them."
- Oscar Wilde, *The Picture of Dorian Gray*

"In order to move on, you must understand why you felt what you did and why you no longer need to feel it."

- **Mitch Albom,** *The Five People You Meet in Heaven*

"Emotion is more powerful than reason. Emotion is the driving force behind thinking and reasoning. Emotional intelligence increases the mind's ability to make positive, brilliant decisions." **- Dr. T.P. Chia**

"Anybody can become angry — that is easy, but to be angry with the right person and to the right degree and at the right time and for the right purpose and in the right way — that is not within everybody's power and is not easy."

- **Aristotle**

At the end of the day, you are the captain of your ship and the driver of your car. Put your emotions back in line so you can reap the best in every situation possible. Often times, when we are tested, it is our response that matters the most. By being in control of your emotions, you can have greater confidence that you are passing life's tests because your responses to the various trials that come will be right.

Choose today to control your emotions and feelings so you can maximize and leverage every opportunity you have to succeed in life, to be happy, and create the life you want.

Action Now
Practice taking action in the area of your emotions, now. Action is powerful. Action in the moment is king. It leaves no room for fear or for perfection.

EMOTION DECLARATIONS

DECLARE: I choose to practice trust on purpose.

What is easy for you to believe about this statement?

What makes it hard or difficult?

Where have you heard this?

List all messaging you have encountered around this.

Are you ready to shift?

Breakthrough Question: Why do I choose to practice trust on purpose?

Breakthrough Action:

DECLARE: I let go of worries and anxieties.

What is easy for you to believe about this statement?

What makes it hard or difficult?

Where have you heard this?

List all the messaging you have encountered around this.

Are you ready to shift?

Breakthrough Question: Why do I let go of worries and anxieties?

Breakthrough Action:

DECLARE: I am emotionally strong and balanced.

What is easy for you to believe about this statement?

What makes it hard or difficult?

Where have you heard this?

List all the messaging you have encountered around this.

Are you ready to shift?

Breakthrough Question: Why am I emotionally strong and balanced?

Breakthrough Action:

DECLARE: I control my emotions while thinking logically and clearly.

What is easy for you to believe about this statement?

What makes it hard or difficult?

Where have you heard this?

List all the messaging you have encountered around this.

Are you ready to shift?

Breakthrough Question: Why do I control my emotions, while thinking logically and clearly?

Breakthrough Action: Practice noticing where you do not feel whole. Note thoughts that would have you feel less than whole. Practice countering those thoughts and replacing them with thoughts in alignment with being whole.

DECLARE: _____

What is easy for you to believe about this statement?

What makes it hard or difficult?

Where have you heard this?

List all the messaging you have encountered around this.

Are you ready to shift?

Breakthrough Question: Are you willing to let go of any negative messaging around this so you can become the fullest, best version of you?

Breakthrough Action: Practice noticing where you do not feel whole. Note thoughts that would have you feel less than whole. Practice countering those thoughts and replacing them with thoughts in alignment with being whole.

Time to Check-In.

You did it! You are working those mental fitness muscles out and will be seeing positive results very soon. Shifting your perspective and digging into why things occur the way they occur for you is challenging—especially when our mental muscles are not accustomed to working out this way.

However, you're doing great!

In the space below, I want you to tell me what you would like to be acknowledged for.

To share, send what you just wrote to our email info@GreatnessRealized.com with the word "Acknowledgement" as the subject line.

6

HEALTH

| **health** — (noun) the state of being free from illness or injury. |

Enough cannot be said about our health. We have one, ONE run at this shot called life. We only have one body, and boy do we push it to the max. We tax, strain, and often neglect our bodies through lack of conditioning and consuming whatever we want. For many of us, the health of our bodies and our overall well-being is low on our priority list. Many of us put ourselves second to low, on the priority list, placing everyone and everything ahead of us.

From unhealthy eating patterns to lack of water consumption, from not getting enough sleep to eating too much junk or fast food, from smoking, consuming too much alcohol, drugs, or sex—all can be detrimental to our health and bodies when not monitored appropriately.

The notion that our bodies are invincible, that nothing can or will go wrong, and that we might not face challenges in our health is flawed. Our opportunity is to shift our thinking in a way that honors who we are and our bodies, by choosing to take care of ourselves. This body, this model, is the only one were given and we want it to function properly for as long as we are alive. There is nothing worse than having an alert mind and a body that is failing because we did not choose to take care of it.

When we flat out fail to condition our bodies with regularity, the impact of this choice can lead us down unsavory paths.

Nugget: Allow me to save you years of potential therapy, time, money, soul searching, and more. Your health, exercise, money goals, and dreams are not failing. Your desire to be greater than the resistance you currently face is getting the best of you. Your desire to deal with and discipline your own temper-tantrum is beating you right now. Why? Because you lack *discipline*. You lack the discipline necessary to check your temper-tantrums. You lack the *self-discipline* to resist what is currently getting the best of you. You are under-performing in your health goals and other areas of life because you lack *discipline*. Like oxygen and hydrogen are the key building blocks for existence, discipline is the key building block for achievement and behavior reinforcement. Discipline is a critical component of mental fitness.

Health has long been a key element for life, yet it seems to come with a struggle at times. Let's gain some additional perspectives on health from the following:

"Moderation. Small helpings. Sample a little bit of everything. These are the secrets of happiness and good health." **- Julia Child**

"In order to change, we must be sick and tired of being sick and tired." **- Unknown**

"You can't enjoy wealth if you are not in good health."
- Unknown

"Your body hears everything your mind says."
- Naomi Judd

"Happiness is the highest form of health." **- Dali Lama**

"The human body is the best picture of the human soul."
- Anthony Robbins

"Our bodies are our gardens — our wills are our gardeners." **- William Shakespeare**

"The only way to keep your health is to eat what you don't want, drink what you don't like, and do what you'd rather not." **- Mark Twain**

"Having a healthy mind is just as important as having a healthy body." **- Unknown**

"If you think wellness is expensive, try illness."
- Unknown

"He who can believe himself well, will be well." **- Ovid**

"Your body holds deep wisdom. Trust in it. Learn from it. Nourish it. Watch your life transform and be healthy."
- Bella Bleue

"The part can never be well unless the whole is well."
- **Plato**

    Another critical area that is being discussed more often in our current culture is the health and wellness of our minds—our mental fitness. Our minds are powerful hubs that source all we do. Like our bodies, our minds are constantly subjected to the harsh elements of our environments—abuse, depression, stress, anxiety, the spectrum of extreme emotion, substance abuse, our own self-talk (especially if it is negative), and so much more. Our mind flexes to bend and stretch, withstanding and absorbing all that filters through. To the extent that we focus on a matter with heavy repetition, groves and trenches are created in our minds that imprint whatever the thought more permanently.

    Consider this: many studies have linked various diseases to stress. Stress is related to our environments—the way we process, interpret, and internalize the stimuli in that environment. How we process our environment and the stimuli affecting us is a function of our mind.

    There are many other diseases that our minds have processed and filtered over time. Studies have shown that extreme emotions like anger or depression link to various cancers and other diseases. Unforgiveness and bitterness are also cancerous worms that if left over time, eat away at our sanity and yield unhealthy states in the mind and body, leading to disease. It is becoming more common for doctors to ask their patients about grudges or unforgiveness. Some who do not choose to ask these questions straight out will tell stories to their patients if they suspect their patient is dealing with bitterness or unforgiveness, linking the effects those seemingly harmless elements have on the body.

We have to get past the notion that the mind and body are not connected. Everything in our bodies — from the mind, emotions, and spirit — are linked, interwoven, and work for us or against us. Often, our minds have been dealing with issues for years, prior to the body showing any symptom of being in a state of disease.

Some may feel it is easier to govern what you can't see versus what you can. For example, you may find it harder to control a bloody finger that was just cut with a knife while cooking in the kitchen. You may think, *Oh well, it's normal for the body to bleed.* But another perspective would be to exercise caution and focus while cooking in the kitchen with a sharp knife. Not allowing yourself to be distracted while using the knife, or when distractions come, simply setting the knife down.

Do you see the different mind shift? One example was reactive while the other was proactive. Though it is only an example — it's a tangible and practical way of controlling our own environment. One example allows for a looser filter with a reactive foundation, and the other allowed a tighter filter with a proactive foundation.

A tighter filter that is proactive for our minds, bodies, and mental health is completely possible. More people are opting in at the chance to control their environments even more. Social media is a great example of this. On any given platform, we see and pass through our filters, for the exact content we want to see simply by liking, following, or subscribing to content and messaging pumped into us.

Traditional media is another example of this, as many consumers are opting out of cable altogether and moving to subscription-based services to choose exactly what they want to watch. Many people, especially Millennials, have moved away from watching the news, due to the intense negative imagery and stories crafted around what is shown. They only want to consume news that is valuable to them, on their terms. Greater still, many only feel it is news if a story has gone viral—shared or reposted multiple times, flooding their feeds or timelines.

These examples prove that it is not difficult to shift our mindsets from a reactive to a proactive foundation. By doing so, we intentionally create a filtration system for our minds, controlling our environments to allow exactly what we choose into our spaces and limiting what we know is toxic for us.

Like anything, we can shift, say yes, adopt, and opt-in to a concept of change right away. The challenge comes over time, with repetition and building our muscles to support our yes.

To build muscle, it is a constant matter of choice over time. We can choose to filter our media, the places we go, what we eat, our social circles, and more. However, we can also filter our minds by resting and picking places and activities that allow us to release tension. Positive affirmations are fantastic reinforcers to guide our thoughts, shape our beliefs, and interrupt old, broken thoughts that no longer serve, benefit, and work for us.

Action Now
Practice taking action in the area of your health, now. Action is powerful. Action in the moment is king. It leaves no room for fear or for perfection.

HEALTH
DECLARATIONS

DECLARE: I am healthy and I treat my body like the temple it is.

What is easy for you to believe about this statement?

What makes it hard or difficult?

Where have you heard this?

List all messaging you have encountered around this.

Are you ready to shift?

Breakthrough Question: Why am I healthy and why do I treat my body like the temple that it is?

Breakthrough Action: Practice noticing where you do not feel whole. Note thoughts that would have you feel less than whole. Practice countering those thoughts and replacing them with thoughts in alignment with being whole.

DECLARE: Every cell in my body works to keep me healthy.

What is easy for you to believe about this statement?

What makes it hard or difficult?

Where have you heard this?

List all messaging you have encountered around this.

Are you ready to shift?

Breakthrough Question: Why does every cell in my body work to keep me healthy?

Breakthrough Action:

DECLARE: My body knows exactly how to heal itself and get what it needs to do so.

What is easy for you to believe about this statement?

What makes it hard or difficult?

Where have you heard this?

List all messaging you have encountered around this.

Are you ready to shift?

Breakthrough Question: Why does my body know exactly how to heal itself and get what it needs to do so?

Breakthrough Action:

DECLARE: I am grateful for my healthy body.

What is easy for you to believe about this statement?

What makes it hard or difficult?

Where have you heard this?

List all the messaging you have encountered around this.

Are you ready to shift?

Breakthrough Question: Why am I grateful for my healthy body?

Breakthrough Action:

DECLARE: _____

What is easy for you to believe about this statement?

What makes it hard or difficult?

Where have you heard this?

List all the messaging you have encountered around this.

Are you ready to shift?

Breakthrough Question: Are you willing to let go of any negative messaging around this so you can become the fullest, best version of you?

Breakthrough Action:

Time to Check-In.

You did it! You are working those mental fitness muscles out and will be seeing positive results very soon. Shifting your perspective and digging into why things occur the way they occur for you is challenging—especially when our mental muscles are not accustomed to working out this way.

However, you're doing great!

In the space below, I want you to tell me what you would like to be acknowledged for.

To share, send what you just wrote to our email info@GreatnessRealized.com with the word "Acknowledgement" as the subject line.

7
RELATIONSHIPS

|relationships — (noun) the way in which two or more concepts, objects, or people are connected, or the state of being connected.|

Listen, relationships are critical to our lives. For a moment, think about how every area of our lives intersects to some relationship. If we own businesses, we have relationships with key vendors, clients, contractors, and staff. When we go to work, we have relationships with our co-workers, our bosses, people in other departments, and our clients.

When we come home, we have relationships with our significant other, family members, and friends. If we travel, we have informal relationships and associations with the flight attendants and temporary relationships with the person in the next seat. If we're investing, we have a relationship with our broker, financial guide, or our banker. Perhaps we attend a place of worship, then we have a relationship with our pastor, priest, or rabbi. Maybe our health is important to us, and we work out with a personal trainer or only attend a particular teacher's classes for cycling or yoga. Whatever the case may be, relationships connect and intersect in every area of our lives.

No matter how long or short the connection, we are all impacted by relationships.

Whether it is the server at the restaurant, your significant other, child, flight attendant, or customer representative, there is an impact made when we engage in interactions with one another. Because we are consistently engaging in relationship-type interactions, it's important to be mindful of who we connect with, who we choose to be in relationship with, and who we allow to surround us. For example, it is important that you not have a job that is toxic to you—where you feel mistreated working in a negative environment. There is only so much you can take before you eventually bring that toxicity home and into all your other relationships, creating a negative cycle that no one wants to experience.

It is important for you to create the circumstances you need to succeed—and that includes your atmosphere, environment, the circles you are a part of, the clubs and organizations you join, and more. Each are connected and affect how you achieve your goals, if you achieve your goals, and the level of impact by which your goals are achieved. If you are hanging out with people who are always gossiping, you'll always be gossiping. If you hang with people who are not motivated and waste time, chances are that you'll waste time and become unmotivated. We've all heard that you are the sum of the five people you hang around the most. Ultimately, you are the only one who can control your environment, success, and the altitude to which you climb. Make sure you are making careful and exceptional choices when it comes to your relationships, social circles, and the environment you choose to surround yourself with.

Healthy relationships are critical to success. Healthy relationships are vital for growth. Healthy relationships must be the number one thing you are looking for — period. This is non-negotiable, and I'll explain why.

- ➢ Unhealthy relationships will have you depressed or unhappy at work.
- ➢ Unhealthy romantic relationships can result in you missing days at work and will cause your performance to slip.
- ➢ Unhealthy relationships will affect your money and financial goals.
- ➢ Unhealthy relationships will affect your physical, mental, emotional, and spiritual health.
- ➢ Unhealthy relationships will result in your physical appearance looking busted down and less appealing.
- ➢ Unhealthy relationships will cost you friendships, opportunities, and will STEAL YOUR TIME. And let me remind you: you cannot get your time back, you cannot get

your time back, you cannot get your time back!

> Unhealthy relationships will cause you to make poor choices that impact your short and long-term future.

> Unhealthy relationships can cause you to go down roads you never intended to go down. And you'll only realize it one day, long after, looking at yourself like, *Who is this person? How did I get here?* I'll tell you. Poor relationship choices.

And for the record, society does not help. Reality TV and other social media outlets highlight dysfunctional relationships to the point that many of you think they are "goals." Many of us would never realize a healthy relationship if it smacked us in the face because we are knee-deep in dysfunction, thinking this is the way we should function. I'm not a preacher, but I sure am preaching better than y'all are shouting! (I've always wanted to say that.) But seriously, if we have the opportunity to experience a healthy relationship, we think it's too soft, too easy, or that the person doesn't love us because they are not screaming at us. And many people, unfortunately, have never seen examples of healthy relationships in any area of their lives, let alone healthy romantic relationships.

A common trademark for a healthy relationship is learning how to set boundaries. Healthy relationships have positive boundaries—first for yourself and then for others. Healthy relationships require that you deal with your baggage and emotional issues. Self-esteem, self-confidence, self-respect, self-concept, self-control, self-discipline, self-doubt, self-improvement, self-love, self-mastery, self-sabotage, self-worth, and self-talk are all enormous areas of your life that require you to "do the work" and get your SELF together.

The following perspectives are great nuggets to reference when it comes to our relationships:

"The best and most beautiful things in this world cannot be seen or even heard, but must be felt with the heart."
- Helen Keller

"Love always cures people—both the ones who give it and the ones who receive it." **- Karl A. Menninger**

"Have enough courage to trust love one more time and always one more time." **- Maya Angelou**

"Forgiveness is the oil of all relationships." **- Anonymous**

"When you stop expecting people to be perfect, you can like them for who they are." **-Donald Miller**

"They may forget what you said, but the will never forget how you made them feel." **-Carl Buechner**

"People are lonely because they build walls instead of bridges." **- Joseph F Newton**

"You don't develop courage by being happy in your relationships every day. You develop it by surviving in difficult times and challenging adversity." **- Epicurus**

"Constant kindness can accomplish much. As the sun makes ice melt, kindness causes misunderstanding, mistrust, and hostility to evaporate." **- Albert Schweitzer**

"For beautiful eyes, look for the good in others; for beautiful lips, speak only words of kindness; and for poise, walk with the knowledge that you are never alone."
- Audrey Hepburn

"You can make more friends in two months by becoming interested in other people than you can in two years by trying to get other people interested in you."
- Dale Carnegie

"Assumptions are the termites of relationships."
- Henry Winkler

"It is of practical value to learn to like yourself. Since you must spend so much time with yourself you might as well get some satisfaction out of the relationship."
- Norman Vincent Peale

"Lots of people want to ride with you in the limo, but what you want is someone who will take the bus with you when the limo breaks down." **- Oprah Winfrey**

"Keep away from those who try to belittle your ambitions. Small people always do that, but the really great make you believe that you too can be great." **- Mark Twain**

It is possible to have healthy relationships. It is possible to be in positive and uplifting environments. It is possible to have positive self-talk that is not always tearing yourself down. It is possible to not self-sabotage healthy relationships and opportunities that come your way. It is possible to have self-respect for yourself where you don't operate out of the fear of abandonment and rejection, settling for any old thing that comes your way.

Healthy relationships don't have your mood, emotions, and feelings swinging like an orangutan in a tree. They will not have you set up camp in a place called indecision. They will not lack vision, purpose, or intentionality. And my personal favorite, they will not take all day to recognize sunshine, let alone, figure out what to do with it.

Action Now

Practice taking action in your relationships, now. Action is powerful. Action in the moment is king. It leaves no room for fear or for perfection.

RELATIONSHIP DECLARATIONS

DECLARE: I choose to have healthy relationships.

What is easy for you to believe about this statement?

What makes it hard or difficult?

Where have you heard this?

List all the messaging you have encountered around this.

Are you ready to shift?

Breakthrough Question: Why do I choose to have healthy relationships?

Breakthrough Action:

DECLARE: My relationships are filled with respect, trust, honesty, and loyalty.

What is easy for you to believe about this statement?

What makes it hard or difficult?

Where have you heard this?

List all the messaging you have encountered around this.

Are you ready to shift?

Breakthrough Question: Why are my relationships filled with respect, trust, honesty, and loyalty?

Breakthrough Action:

DECLARE: I am dynamic and draw dynamic people to myself.

What is easy for you to believe about this statement?

What makes it hard or difficult?

Where have you heard this?

List all the messaging you have encountered around this.

Are you ready to shift?

Breakthrough Question: Why am I dynamic how do I draw dynamic people to myself?

Breakthrough Action:

DECLARE: I am attracting people to pour into my life connections and resources.

What is easy for you to believe about this statement?

What makes it hard or difficult?

Where have you heard this?

List all the messaging you have encountered around this.

Are you ready to shift?

Breakthrough Question: Why am I attracting people to pour into my life connections and resources?

Breakthrough Action:

DECLARE: _____

What is easy for you to believe about this statement?

What makes it hard or difficult?

Where have you heard this?

List all the messaging you have encountered around this.

Are you ready to shift?

Breakthrough Question: Are you willing to let go of any negative messaging around this so you can become the fullest, best version of you?

Breakthrough Action: Practice noticing where you do not feel whole. Note thoughts that would have you feel less than whole. Practice countering those thoughts and replacing them with thoughts in alignment with being whole.

Time to Check-In.

You did it! You are working those mental fitness muscles out and will be seeing positive results very soon. Shifting your perspective and digging into why things occur the way they occur for you is challenging—especially when our mental muscles are not accustomed to working out this way.

However, you're doing great!

In the space below, I want you to tell me what you would like to be acknowledged for.

To share, send what you just wrote to our email info@GreatnessRealized.com with the word "Acknowledgement" as the subject line.

8

COMMUNICATION

|communication — (noun) the imparting or exchanging of information or news.|

Have you ever had something you wanted to say but didn't know how to say it? Or maybe you were tasked with a writing project to communicate your thoughts and you got stuck and all jammed up? No matter where you are on the spectrum, communication is a constant part of our everyday lives. And we're all too familiar with pains and frustrations of miscommunication. In this chapter, we'll discuss some best practices to keep in mind while communicating.

While we generally know the rules to communication, they are worth noting again. First, keep your thoughts concise. We all have times when we "think out loud" but overall, communication has a point, so (PSA) hurry up and get to yours. We've all been around certain people who go on and on and on, like the never-ending story. But people get lost in long communication because we are trained to search and listen for the meaning.

While you are working on being concise, remember to be complete—by communicating complete thoughts, not half thoughts. For example, if you constantly talk in fragments or phrases, then ask the person you're chatting with if they know what you mean (just know that they probably have no clue!). You have to talk and convey your thoughts in complete sentences if you want to be understood. It is ridiculous to expect others to assume what you mean in order to understand you.

Use color appropriately. We are wired to be drawn to vivid imagery painted by our words. Colorful words peak our imagination to visualize what's being shared, bring us deeper into the conversation, and create a stronger connection. If you are sharing a story, definitely use color.

Something we all know, but often struggle with, is being clear. Perhaps we are thinking about how our message will be received or what others will think about us. Maybe we work on crafting our message in a way that pleases others, and in the process, our message loses clarity and impact because it is watered down and muddled. This only causes frustration. Be intentional and be clear.

This is a great moment to interject some perspective from others you may know on communication:

"You never know when a moment and a few sincere words can have an impact on life." **- Zig Ziglar**

"I speak to everyone in the same way, whether he is the garbage man or the president of the university."
- Albert Einstein

"Don't be embarrassed by your failures. Learn from them and start again." **- Sir Richard Branson**

"Be sincere, be brief, be seated." **- Franklin D. Roosevelt**

"The way we communicate with others and with ourselves ultimately determines the quality of our lives."
– Anthony Robbins

"The single biggest problem in communication is the illusion it has taken place." **- George Bernard Shaw**

"Communication — the human connection — is the key to personal and career success." **– Paul Meyer**

"When the trust account is high, communication is easy, instant, and effective. **– Stephen Covey**

"Nothing lowers the level of conversation more than raising the voice." **- Stanley Horowitz**

"Your ability to communicate is an important tool in the pursuit of your goals, whether it is with your family, your co-workers, or your clients and customers." **- Les Brown**

Let's go back to a moment when you had something you wanted to share but had a hard time getting it to come out. It's not that you didn't know what to say. It was more that you didn't know if you could share what you wanted to with the person you were talking with. A major key to communication (whether in front of a group or in one-on-one interaction) is that you have to be comfortable with your message and what you are sharing. Let's say you are wanting to communicate with someone close to you and you are hesitant to share (and you've noticed this has become a pattern with this person), you have to wonder if you are *supposed* to share with them. Meaning, is this person trustworthy? Do they really have your best interest at heart? Who is it that you are really communicating with—them or their representative?

Not everything should be shared with everyone. And even then, there are just some things you never share. That's what journals are for—to process and filter your own thoughts and share things you don't yet think you can share with anyone. When you feel like you can't share something with someone specific (and again, this is something you consistently feel about this person over time), this is a potential warning, a red flag that you should notice and take note of. If nothing has changed on your end, perhaps something has shifted on theirs. There could be many reasons why. Until you have clarity, proceed with caution.

You can also ask yourself the following questions: How are you communicating? Are you pushy? Do you always have to talk? Are you demanding or rude? Do you interrupt or cut others off when they are talking? Do you talk over others? Or, are you a kind communicator? Are you sensitive to the ebbs and flows of communication and are you able to read the audience or individual you're communicating with? Your communication has a cadence and channel by which all your messages are sent and received by your recipient.

No matter what's happening around you, challenge yourself to communicate from a channel and a foundation of love.

Love does not always agree with others, it does not keep a record of wrong and right like a scorecard, it is not judgmental—it's simply *love*. Love is a constant, a guide, a North Star if you will. When becoming intentional with your communication and making love the place from which all your messages are sent, your communication with those around you will dramatically improve.

Action Now

Practice taking action toward healthy communication, now. Action is powerful. Action in the moment is king. It leaves no room for fear or for perfection.

COMMUNICATION DECLARATIONS

DECLARE: I communicate with love.

What is easy for you to believe about this statement?

What makes it hard or difficult?

Where have you heard this?

List all the messaging you have encountered around this.

Are you ready to shift?

Breakthrough Question: Why do I communicate with love?

Breakthrough Action:

DECLARE: I communicate clearly and effectively.

What is easy for you to believe about this statement?

What makes it hard or difficult?

Where have you heard this?

List all the messaging you have encountered around this.

Are you ready to shift?

Breakthrough Question: Why do I communicate clearly and effectively?

Breakthrough Action:

DECLARE: I am a natural born communicator.

What is easy for you to believe about this statement?

What makes it hard or difficult?

Where have you heard this?

List all the messaging you have encountered around this.

Are you ready to shift?

Breakthrough Question: Why am I a natural born communicator?

Breakthrough Action:

DECLARE: I communicate with others through writing, publishing, and speaking.

What is easy for you to believe about this statement?

What makes it hard or difficult?

Where have you heard this?

List all the messaging you have encountered around this.

Are you ready to shift?

Breakthrough Question: Why do I communicate with others through writing, publishing, and speaking?

Breakthrough Action:

DECLARE: _____

What is easy for you to believe about this statement?

What makes it hard or difficult?

Where have you heard this?

List all the messaging you have encountered around this.

Are you ready to shift?

Breakthrough Question: Are you willing to let go of any negative messaging around this so you can become the fullest, best version of you?

Breakthrough Action: Practice noticing where you do not feel whole. Note thoughts that would have you feel less than whole. Practice countering those thoughts and replacing them with thoughts in alignment with being whole.

Time to Check-In.

You did it! You are working those mental fitness muscles out and will be seeing positive results very soon. Shifting your perspective and digging into why things occur the way they occur for you is challenging—especially when our mental muscles are not accustomed to working out this way.

However, you're doing great!

In the space below, I want you to tell me what you would like to be acknowledged for.

To share, send what you just wrote to our email info@GreatnessRealized.com with the word "Acknowledgement" as the subject line.

9

BUSINESS | CAREER

|business — (noun) a person's regular occupation, profession, or trade.|

|career — (noun) an occupation undertaken for a significant period of a person's life.|

Our career or business is what we do with over two-thirds of our lives. It is completely normal to want and desire success in our work. The outcome and value of our careers and businesses comes in the form of money. This tool is something we all want enough of and the definition of "enough" varies greatly from person to person.

We want enough to have the life we envision in our mind's eye. We want enough to provide for our families. We want enough to partake in experiences and travel that enhances and enriches our souls. This concept of "enough" is extremely important to each of us, according to our definitions. Before we get too deep, let's get expert reinforcement and perspective:

"The most common way people give up their power is by thinking they don't have any." **– Alice Walker**

"If you don't feel it, flee from it. Go where you are celebrated, not merely tolerated." **- Paul F. Davis**

"Create the environment you need for success."
– Welcome Sarah

"The future depends on what you do today."
– Mahatma Gandhi

"I am not a product of my circumstances. I am a product of my decisions." **- Stephen Covey**

"It's never too late to be what you might have been."
- George Eliot

"There is no passion to be found playing small—in settling for a life that is less than the one you are capable of living."
- Nelson Mandela

"If it scares you, it might be a good thing to try."
– Seth Godin

"Too many of us are not living our dreams because we are living our fears." **– Les Brown**

"The best revenge is massive success." **- Frank Sinatra**

"Dreams are extremely important. You can't do it unless you imagine it." **- George Lucas**

"Desire! That's the one secret of every man's career. Not education. Not being born with hidden talents. Desire."
- Johnny Carson

"If you can DREAM it, you can DO it." **- Walt Disney**

By now, you should be understanding, even more, the importance of your mindset, words, and speaking positively over every area of your life. This practice is a supercharged fertilizer to creating exactly what you want to see. But I would like to emphasize this point again. Often, people think that all that is necessary in this practice is to merely speak what you want, over and over.

Speaking and declaring can be a strong 50% of the equation. But the other half of the equation, which I don't want you to be misled on, is that you must *act*. You must take action and do your part in whatever you are declaring. The doing portion at 50% plus what you are speaking at 50% equals your 100% result.

I'm emphasizing this point because oftentimes I have people share with me that they have declared affirmations until they are blue the face, yet nothing has moved the needle. Others shared that although they acted, their mindset was still negative and saw little results from their actions.

Your words fuel your faith. They fuel your belief. They feed your thoughts. They stir you up on the inside to pursue what is possible with your life.

What you are speaking can come true, can occur, and can become your reality. But it takes both declaration and action to move the needle of results. While some of you may know this already, it is so important to understand; my desire is for you to *overstand*, especially as it relates to your money and your coin.

A friend drilled this concept into me about money and I love it to this day. Every dollar is a representation of every hope and dream you have. It is a measurement of how you are doing. Are you or are you not achieving what you desire? Whether you are working in corporate America or you are an entrepreneur, whether you have built a company and have a team of your own or you're working as a solopreneur—the principle still applies to the moves you are making. Pop-culture icon Cardi B. has a song stating, "I make money moves" and whether you know it or not, you make money moves every day as well.

Whatever corporation you work for, the choices you make—to accept a position, to look for a new position, to remain where you are, to pursue a raise, to add value to your organization, to solve a problem, to disengage with your organization and still remain there with a bad attitude—all impact and directly affect YOU. These choices all affect your assent or decent on the corporate ladder. They affect where you start, they affect your happiness, your quality of life, your time with your family, what you get to experience, your options, your hopes, your dreams, your plans, your ambition, your sanity, and your money!

If you are an entrepreneur or solopreneur—your industry, your familiarity with your industry, knowledge, contacts, ability to fail fast, ability to be resilient, ability to create meaningful connections and network, your resources, your money to invest in your business, business plan, marketing plan, team, contractors, plan to scale, the problems you solve and the value you bring—all impact you and the moves you can make now and in the future. Your choices, your sacrifices, your dedication, your foolishness, your mentors, your ability to learn and unlearn, all directly impact you and your options.

We live in such an "instant" society—a society with people who are quick to forget there is a process to their progress. You can start a company or climb the corporate ladder but there is still a process to your progress. Do not forget that action is the process that provides the progress you desperately seek.

Now, more than ever, it appears our thirst is out of alignment. We thirst for the result without taking the action steps necessary to reach the outcome. We search for shortcuts that only cut us short of all that is already ours from the very foundation of time. We sellout instead of selling out to the work, the goal, the drive, and the process that yields the progress.

Move the needle. Do the work. It doesn't even matter where—don't get caught up in the minutia of being in corporate or being an entrepreneur or a being a business owner or starting your own thing. If you are caught up in titles, then you will miss out on the point. Not everyone is meant to be an entrepreneur or a business owner. Entrepreneurship is a delicate balance that will test your sanity and put you face-to-face with your fears; it is not at all for the faint in heart or if you have a weak stomach. In contrast, not everyone is meant to be working in corporate America. However, while you figure this out, I am a strong advocate to have your feet in both places, allowing your corporate position to fund and invest in your entrepreneurial endeavors.

So, let's tie this together. Declarations seek and hinge on clarity. How can you DECLARE what is not clear? We have firmly established that work is essential, no matter the type, and shares breath and space with your coin, opportunities, and possibilities. It is only now that we can begin to water what we see with our words, giving life to that vision and commanding the framework of success in our career and business through our words.

While you may not have built a home yourself, you can go on Google and see what a new home looks like when it is being framed out. When the foundation and frame are being set, a home is given its shape. Rooms are being outlined and areas of the home are becoming identifiable. Usually, the step after framing is adding sheetrock to the posts to continue to make the finished vision of the home a reality.

In a similar manner, your words have the same effect. When you begin to speak over your career or business you are framing out what you want to see. (Keep in mind, it makes no difference if you are speaking positive or negative words—the principle remains the same.) But as you begin to speak success, connections, resources, favor, joy, clients, ease, etc. over your life—your mental fitness begins to acclimate to the conditions of what you are saying. Your belief begins to align, your work ethic starts to form, and you will begin to see the manifestation of what you've said. Because you can shape the outcome, success, and direction of your work—choose to nurture your success with words of life and affirmation. (And if you are stuck with what declarations to proclaim, this book contains several options for you to choose from.)

Action Now
Practice taking action in the area of your career or business growth, now. Action is powerful. Action in the moment is king. It leaves no room for fear or for perfection.

CAREER | BUSINESS
DECLARATIONS

DECLARE: I value who I am and what I do.

What is easy for you to believe about this statement?

What makes it hard or difficult?

Where have you heard this?

List all the messaging you have encountered around this.

Are you ready to shift?

Breakthrough Question: Why do I value who I am and what I do?

Breakthrough Action:

DECLARE: I am passionate about my work and all I do.

What is easy for you to believe about this statement?

What makes it hard or difficult?

Where have you heard this?

List all the messaging you have encountered around this.

Are you ready to shift?

Breakthrough Question: Why am I passionate about my work and all I do?

Breakthrough Action:

DECLARE: I am the best at what I do.

What is easy for you to believe about this statement?

What makes it hard or difficult?

Where have you heard this?

List all messaging you have encountered around this.

Are you ready to shift?

Breakthrough Question: Why am I the best at what I do?

Breakthrough Action:

DECLARE: Quality clients are attracted to do business with me and pay well.

What is easy for you to believe about this statement?

What makes it hard or difficult?

Where have you heard this?

List all the messaging you have encountered around this.

Are you ready to shift?

Breakthrough Question: Why are quality clients attracted to do business with me and pay well?

Breakthrough Action:

DECLARE: _____

What is easy for you to believe about this statement?

What makes it hard or difficult?

Where have you heard this?

List all the messaging you have encountered around this.

Are you ready to shift?

Breakthrough Question: Are you willing to let go of any negative messaging around this so you can become the fullest, best version of you?

Breakthrough Action: Practice noticing where you do not feel whole. Note thoughts that would have you feel less than whole. Practice countering those thoughts and replacing them with thoughts in alignment with being whole.

Time to Check-In.

You did it! You are working those mental fitness muscles out and will be seeing positive results very soon. Shifting your perspective and digging into why things occur the way they occur for you is challenging—especially when our mental muscles are not accustomed to working out this way.

However, you're doing great!

In the space below, I want you to tell me what you would like to be acknowledged for.

To share, send what you just wrote to our email info@GreatnessRealized.com with the word "Acknowledgement" as the subject line.

10

MONEY | WEALTH

| **money** — (noun) a current medium of exchange in the form of coins and banknotes collectively. |

| **wealth** — (noun) an abundance of valuable possessions or money. |

Perhaps one of the most sought-after constructs is the *idea* of money and wealth, followed closely by the *tangibility* of obtaining money and wealth. Most can agree that money and wealth are tools that open doors, create opportunities, and provide access.

It is said that most problems in life are solved by time or money. To reiterate the powerful thought from my friend highlighted in the previous chapter, money and wealth are comprised of dollars, which represent every hope and dream you have. You get to decide how you spend and allocate each denominator, hope, and dream. Money and wealth are tools—mere measurements of value—

representing how well you are (or are not) achieving what you desire.

Yes, wealth can be comprised of a great many things—love, peace, happiness, health—all of which have merit. However, for the purposes of this chapter, we will be looking at wealth primarily through a monetary lens.

There are many cultures across the globe who talk about money—openly and freely—as commonly as Americans would talk about eating. Monetary discussions in other cultures are casual conversations, rarely is there any taboo or secrecy around it. Salary, the cost of acquisition, purchasing homes, cars, businesses, to how much money a person has on them presently are all common topics in conversation. In contrast, this is not the same experience for most Americans. Rather, our experiences around open money and wealth conversations are limited. Most Americans are not comfortable discussing things like salary and feel it taboo to do so.

To be generous, less than 5% of the population discusses generational wealth. Most Americans are frivolous spenders, wasting dollars, hopes, and dreams, or their leverage to position themselves and their families into the juicy places they desperately desire to occupy. Before we move too far ahead, let's explore the thoughts others have around money below.

"Too many people spend money they haven't earned to buy things they don't want to impress people they don't like." **– Will Rogers**

"Every day is a bank account, and time is our currency. No one is rich, no one is poor, we've got 24 hours each."
- **Christopher Rice**

"It's how you deal with failure that determines how you achieve success." – **David Feherty**

"An investment in knowledge pays the best interest."
– **Benjamin Franklin**

"I will tell you the secret to getting rich on Wall Street. You try to be greedy when others are fearful. And you try to be fearful when others are greedy." – **Warren Buffett**

"Opportunity is missed by most people because it is dressed in overalls and looks like work." – **Thomas Edison**

"What we really want to do is what we are really meant to do. When we do what we are meant to do, money comes to us, doors open for us, we feel useful and the work we do feels like play to us." - **Julia Cameron**

"Many people take no care of their money till they come nearly to the end of it, and others do just the same with their time." – **Johann Wolfgang von Goethe**

"Formal education will make you a living; self-education will make you a fortune." – **Jim Rohn**

"Empty pockets never held anyone back. Only empty heads and empty hearts can do that." – **Norman V. Peale**

"Innovation distinguishes between a leader and a follower." **- Steve Jobs**

"The real measure of your wealth is how much you'd be worth if you lost all your money." **- Anonymous**

"Money is a terrible master but an excellent servant."
- P.T. Barnum

"I'm a great believer in luck, and I find the harder I work the more I have of it." **- Thomas Jefferson**

"Wealth is the ability to fully experience life."
- Henry David Thoreau

Let's continue to lay the foundation and framework around money and wealth. If we were in chemistry class, we would say money and wealth have a neutral charge—meaning they take on the characteristics of their possessor.

Money and wealth are simply tools at our disposal. Inherently, money and wealth are neither good nor bad.

Imagine, a positive person has wealth and they often donate their money to causes and charities they support. We'd say that person is "rich," and our feelings and sentiments associated with them would most likely be positive. Furthermore, we would likely say positive and complimentary remarks about that individual. In contrast, if a wealthy individual does not donate *any* of their money to philanthropic causes or charities (and is an overall jerk of a person), one might say they are stingy, a Scrooge, rich, or mean. Slowly, we begin to label their money as "bad" or with a negative sentiment, simply because the person who is in possession of it has a negative persona.

Digging deeper, money and wealth have no value attached to them. Money is a metric, a unit of measurement that is used to exchange for something else of perceived value. Period. They are neutral and free of association. However, we often rush to assign value to money and simultaneously, assign value to ourselves. We DECLARE our value with how much money we have or will have someday, forgetting that money is only a tool. (If you can catch this, it will save you thousands of dollars in future therapy. If you don't understand just yet, stick with me for a moment — you will thank me later!) I guarantee, in some way, you've attached your worth to the construct of money. And don't feel bad — you're not the only one. We've all done it.

But let me ask you this: In what circumstance (other than with money) have your tools or resources been limited? When was the last time you were in a classroom setting where the teacher told you to only bring one pen because that would be all you would need? Or to not use your computer to take notes, because that tool was obsolete? *Do you see how ridiculous that sounds? How that would not happen?*

Yet, here we are, limiting ourselves to only a few tools when it comes to our money when we could have more, and often need more! But we often believe, "You can only have one hope or wish today, so that's all the tools you'll be needing to realize your hope or dream." *Are you kidding?* Can we not get some more tools here? Is there a crazy-random-tool-shortage-plot-working-against-only-you?! The truth is, there are unlimited tools waiting for us to swoop them up and put them to use — working toward our hopes and dreams — causing us to realize them in actual, tangible form.

Your money and wealth mindset may have told you (1) you are not worthy of money or wealth, (2) you are not worthy of the money or wealth you desire, (3) there is a crazy-random-money-and-wealth-shortage-plot-working-against-only-you AND the money and wealth pot only has one more dollar! And sadly, you believed it! We've all believed these crazy, absurd lies — all because our money and wealth mindsets are out of alignment.

Instead of flexing our muscles back at these lies, showing them just how fit our money mindset is, we curl up in the corner to take a beating — DAILY! Imagine the best boxer or fighter you've ever known or heard of. They are pretty incredible, right? You've seen them in action or have heard they are a legend and want NO part of them, right? Whoever you just thought of, imagine them having you in a corner, curled up in a ball, going nuts, beating you up. Got the visual? Feel the pain? Exactly! This is how these lies are whooping your tail, daily — and notice yourself again, in the corner, in a ball. No muscle. Not flexing. Not moving.

DECLARE

We've got to do better. Like, get me to the ER better. However, if we would just start going to the gym of Mental Fitness for Money and Wealth, we would be able to flex back and whoop tail so much faster. At that point, there would be no need to thank me, as you would be thanking YOU—your life situation would be thanking you, and I imagine those who love you would be thanking you as well.

The affirmations and the work contained in this book as a whole and specifically around money and wealth are priceless. Consider this your 7-day free pass to the gym of Mental Fitness for Money and Wealth. Get yourself to the gym and start delivering blows of your own to the lies that have you bound, crippled, and in horrible shape. It's time to win in the area of wealth and money.

Nugget: OPERATE AS IF YOU ALREADY HAVE THE MONEY YOU WANT NOW. When you can settle this in yourself and relate to yourself as already having what you desire, your desires will show up and become tangible. This nugget is true across every aspect of your life, and especially every area highlighted in this book. The fact of the matter is this: You already have all that you desire and more, NOW. The gap you are missing is the simple fact that you are not relating to yourself and seeing yourself as having it *now*.

Action Now
Practice taking action in the area of your finances, now. Action is powerful. Action in the moment is king. It leaves no room for fear or for perfection.

MONEY | WEALTH
DECLARATIONS

DECLARE: I am prosperous.

What is easy for you to believe about this statement?

What makes it hard or difficult?

Where have you heard this?

List all the messaging you have encountered around this.

Are you ready to shift?

Breakthrough Question: Why am I prosperous?

Breakthrough Action: Practice noticing where you do not feel whole. Note thoughts that would have you feel less than whole. Practice countering those thoughts and replacing them with thoughts in alignment with being whole.

DECLARE: I have an abundance of time and money.

What is easy for you to believe about this statement?

What makes it hard or difficult?

Where have you heard this?

List all the messaging you have encountered around this.

Are you ready to shift?

Breakthrough Question: Why do I have an abundance of time and money?

Breakthrough Action: Practice noticing where you do not feel whole. Note thoughts that would have you feel less than whole. Practice countering those thoughts and replacing them with thoughts in alignment with being whole.

DECLARE: I am attracting health, wealth, and happiness from all sides, daily.

What is easy for you to believe about this statement?

What makes it hard or difficult?

Where have you heard this?

List all messaging you have encountered around this.

Are you ready to shift?

Breakthrough Question: Why am I attracting health, wealth, and happiness from all sides, daily?

Breakthrough Action: Practice noticing where you do not feel whole. Note thoughts that would have you feel less than whole. Practice countering those thoughts and replacing them with thoughts in alignment with being whole.

DECLARE: People love to give me money.

What is easy for you to believe about this statement?

What makes it hard or difficult?

Where have you heard this?

List all the messaging you have encountered around this.

Are you ready to shift?

Breakthrough Question: Why do people love to give me money?

Breakthrough Action:

DECLARE: _____

What is easy for you to believe about this statement?

What makes it hard or difficult?

Where have you heard this?

List all messaging you have encountered around this.

Are you ready to shift?

Breakthrough Question: Are you willing to let go of any negative messaging around this so you can become the fullest, best version of you?

Breakthrough Action: Practice noticing where you do not feel whole. Note thoughts that would have you feel less than whole. Practice countering those thoughts and replacing them with thoughts in alignment with being whole.

Time to Check-In.

You did it! You are working those mental fitness muscles out and will be seeing positive results very soon. Shifting your perspective and digging into why things occur the way they occur for you is challenging—especially when our mental muscles are not accustomed to working out this way.

However, you're doing great!

In the space below, I want you to tell me what you would like to be acknowledged for.

To share, send what you just wrote to our email info@GreatnessRealized.com with the word "Acknowledgement" as the subject line.

11

SPEAKING

| **speaking** — (noun) the action of conveying information or expressing one's thoughts and feelings in spoken language. |

According to Forbes Magazine, only about 10% of people love public speaking, while the other 80-90% are either terribly afraid or have some anxiety or nerves when it comes to speaking in public.

What would you say is the most powerful tool you have access to? Hopefully, your voice made one of the top three in the list.

Your voice is powerful as it activates your thoughts, taking the creative matter of your thinking and molding it into tangible items you can hold and feel. In the simplest form, your voice allows you to communicate what you wish to eat from a restaurant, stories with family and friends, and expressions of pain, pleasure, laughter, and more.

At your core—at the essence of your being—you are creative. You can speak into being what does not yet exist.

Children are molded by words.

We are taught in school through words, messages, and theories we are meant to comprehend.

We've all heard the phrases, "Sticks and stones may break my bones, but words will never hurt me," and "Life and death are in the power of your tongue."

Simply put, our words have power.

"Speech is power: speech is to persuade, to convert, to compel." - **Ralph Waldo Emerson**

"The right word may be effective, but no word was ever as effective as a rightly timed pause." - **Mark Twain**

"The kindest word in all the world is the unkind word, unsaid." - **Unknown**

"The trouble with talking too fast is you may say something you haven't thought of yet." - **Ann Landers**

"The easiest way to save face is to keep the lower half shut." - **Unknown**

"The words you choose to say are just as important as the decision to speak." - **Unknown**

"Not even the fastest horse can catch a word spoken in anger." **- Chinese Proverb**

Even the premise of this book is founded on the act of engaging your voice to DECLARE positivity over your life. To speak well, to "till the soil of your mind," so that the goals, dreams, desires, or "harvest" will begin to become visible.

Engaging our voice is powerful because, by doing so, we shift the atmospheres of our lives. Through engaging our voice, we take control of our narrative — our story — and relinquish the plight of victimization (or playing the victim) and determine how our story will go. Our voice interrupts and disrupts the stories of our lives that are on auto-pilot.

Belief stems from what we hear and observe. That's why many of us are messed up in our thinking because we have been washed in the water of the words of those who don't have our best in mind. Those who should have meant you well, protected you, and kept you from harm — yet instead, bathed you in the dirty and polluted water of their words.

Many of our struggles come from the pollution others have spoken into our lives. Negative words will leach onto our identity, attempting to tear it down, brick by brick.

Toxic words create their own playlist in our minds, looping on repeat when we consciously think of a person or memory that triggers whatever was spoken. But the biggest kickers are the negative playlists that play *subconsciously.*

Just like the broken tapes we talked about in Chapter 1, we must remove these broken thought patterns looping in our minds that are no longer serving us or others.

What we choose to speak to others and DECLARE over ourselves has incredible impact and power to shape, tear down, build up, soothe, heal, and more.

Studies show that when plants are spoken to, they grow even more. In the same way, when we speak positive and encouraging words to children, they grow, perform, and cope better than children who are spoken negatively to. Whatever we are speaking over them, we are framing and setting the foundation for what they will believe and how they will respond.

It is so important that we become more cognizant of our words, the power we have in speaking, and the impact we carry. It is crucial that we become mindful of what we speak, say, and DECLARE — everything that comes out of our mouth.

Our words are nothing more than verbalized thought.

All of us, at our core, are creators and have the ability to create. Therefore, we really have to be aware of our words and their impact.

Choose to align your thoughts and words. Choose to speak positively over your life and the lives of others.

Action Now

Practice taking action in the area of your speech, now. Action is powerful—and so is your voice. Action in the moment is king. It leaves no room for fear or for perfection.

SPEAKING
DECLARATIONS

DECLARE: I speak life.

What is easy for you to believe about this statement?

What makes it hard or difficult?

Where have you heard this?

List all the messaging you have encountered around this.

Are you ready to shift?

Breakthrough Question: Why do I communicate with others through writing, publishing, and speaking?

Breakthrough Action:

DECLARE: I speak with power, ease, passion, and conviction.

What is easy for you to believe about this statement?

What makes it hard or difficult?

Where have you heard this?

List all the messaging you have encountered around this.

Are you ready to shift?

Breakthrough Question: Why do I communicate with others through writing, publishing, and speaking? Or, why do I want to start?

Breakthrough Action:

DECLARE: I am a highly sought-after speaker.

What is easy for you to believe about this statement?

What makes it hard or difficult?

Where have you heard this?

List all the messaging you have encountered around this.

Are you ready to shift?

Breakthrough Question: Why do I communicate with others through writing, publishing, and speaking? Or, why do I want to?

Breakthrough Action:

DECLARE: I am well-compensated speaker.

What is easy for you to believe about this statement?

What makes it hard or difficult?

Where have you heard this?

List all the messaging you have encountered around this.

Are you ready to shift?

Breakthrough Question: Why do I communicate with others through writing, publishing, and speaking? Why do I desire to?

Breakthrough Action:

DECLARE: _____

What is easy for you to believe about this statement?

What makes it hard or difficult?

Where have you heard this?

List all messaging you have encountered around this.

Are you ready to shift?

Breakthrough Question: Why do I communicate with others through writing, publishing, and speaking? Or, why will I start?

Breakthrough Action:

Time to Check-In.

You did it! You are working those mental fitness muscles out and will be seeing positive results very soon. Shifting your perspective and digging into why things occur the way they occur for you is challenging—especially when our mental muscles are not accustomed to working out this way.

However, you're doing great!

In the space below, I want you to tell me what you would like to be acknowledged for.

To share, send what you just wrote to our email info@GreatnessRealized.com with the word "Acknowledgement" as the subject line.

12

SPIRITUALITY

|spirituality — (noun) the quality of being concerned with the human spirit or soul as opposed to material or physical things.|

Believe it or not, spirituality is critical for all of us. It is what grounds us, shapes our world view, impacts how we treat other people, and affects how we care for ourselves and our families.

Having a foundation of spiritually grounds us and helps us to focus through the various trials and challenges we face in life.

But have you ever noticed the conversation about spirituality can be weird and feel sticky?

Spirituality is morphing into a multitude of meanings and symbols, and it seems that everyone has their own definition, no matter who you ask.

Here are some concepts regarding spirituality that I feel are important to highlight and distinguish:

1. There is a difference between spirituality and religion. More often than not, when applied, religion tends to have a legalistic feel to it. Spirituality, on the other hand, tends to be more relational, it has a more personal feel, and is generally founded in love. If we could all adopt the practice of operating in love—both in giving and receiving love—what we could build and create from this place of unity would be a force of power and wholeness to be reckoned with.

2. There is such a thing as being imbalanced. Meaning, you are so entrenched in your own beliefs that a state of paralysis sets in and your actions are no longer in alignment with what you say you believe. For example: Say you have a belief in having faith for those less fortunate to get assistance (water, food, shelter). Have you ever thought that maybe you should *do* something about it, rather than waiting for someone else to do something? (This is a simple, but generalized example to show, when magnified, how we can become paralyzed, not embodying and acting on what we believe.)

My mom used to have a story hanging in her office and as a child, whenever I would visit her at work, I would read it. I'm not sure why I loved this short story so much at such a young age, but

I think it best illustrates my point. It's a story about Everybody, Somebody, Anybody, and Nobody.

This is a little story about four people named Everybody, Somebody, Anybody, and Nobody. There was an important job to be done and Everybody was sure that Somebody would do it. Anybody could have done it, but Nobody did it. Somebody got angry about that because it was Everybody's job. Everybody thought that Anybody could do it, but Nobody realized that Everybody wouldn't do it. It ended up that Everybody blamed Somebody when Nobody did what Anybody could have done.

– Author Unknown

3. Spirituality, by nature, can be a reflective shining light on opportunities to improve ourselves, should we be willing.

Having a mirror reflecting our areas of growth and where we have room for development is essential for all of our lives. Our whole life is one big growth cycle (as evident by our getting older). Growth is not something we should stiff-arm; rather, an invitation to evolve into a better version of who we are. One practice or perspective I value is the ability to practice being open to others as teachers.

We can all see various things about each other that sometimes we do not see ourselves. I find that I grow more when I am open to others as a reflection and allow them to show me reflections of myself. Sometimes, those reflections are not always correct — but even in those moments, I still gained the practice and the intentional muscle-building work to be open to grow and receive valuable reflections from those around me and those I encounter.

4. Spirituality dictates alignment. It's easy, without a spiritual base, to not have our thoughts, beliefs, words, and actions line up. Spirituality lends itself to discipline and greater congruency. Moral codes, ethical standards, and integrity all have roots in spirituality, even if your daily practice is nothing more than love.

5. Practicing core tenants of what you believe causes you to be present in your life, relationships, and interactions — instead of simply going through the motions. Being present creates space for meaningful and genuine connections. It's ironic how we, as people — little human finite beings — operate as if we have all the time in the world. We either spend way too much time in our past or our future but fail to see the beauty of the only real moment we have which is NOW. Time is now, and our gift is the present. Beauty comes in learning to allow your presence to rest in the present gift of each moment you find yourself in, instead of being physically present and fully experiencing the beauty and connection each moment is offering you.

Mother Teresa was a great example of healthy spirituality. She was a huge advocate and proponent of love. Her core tenant was love, she practiced love, she shared love, and she spread love wherever she went. She was moved with compassion and for her, love was at the heart of her spirituality.

The following quotes provide some additional perspective on spirituality.

"He who is filled with love is filled with God Himself."
- Saint Augustine

"The spiritual journey is the unlearning of fear and the acceptance of love." **- Marianne Williamson**

"I choose gentleness… Noting is won by force. I choose to be gentle. If I raise my voice, may it be only in praise. If I clench my fist, may it be only in prayer. If I make a demand, may it be only of myself." **- Max Lucado**

"If a man is to live, he must be all alive, body, soul, mind, heart, spirit." **- Thomas Merton**

"Realize deeply that the present moment is all you have. Make the now the primary focus of your life."
- Eckhart Tolle

"Being at ease with not knowing is crucial for answers to come to you." **- Eckhart Tolle**

"Nurture great thoughts, for you will never go higher than your thoughts." **- Benjamin Disraeli**

"If you judge people, you have no time to love them."
- Mother Teresa

"Nothing is unless our thinking makes it so."
- William Shakespeare

"It is not in the stars to hold our destiny but in ourselves."
- William Shakespeare

"It is better in prayer to have a heart without words than words without a heart." **- Mahatma Gandhi**

"Physical strength can never permanently withstand the impact of spiritual force." **- Franklin D Roosevelt**

"When you arise in the morning think of what a privilege it is to be alive, to think, to enjoy, to love."
- Marcus Aurelius

Spirituality, in some form, is woven into our lives and how we see and interact with the world and those around us.

Action Now

Practice taking action in the area of your spirituality, now. Action is powerful. Action in the moment is king. It leaves no room for fear or for perfection.

SPIRITUALITY
DECLARATIONS

DECLARE: I am enough.

What is easy for you to believe about this statement?

What makes it hard or difficult?

Where have you heard this?

List all the messaging you have encountered around this.

Are you ready to shift?

Breakthrough Question: Why am I enough?

Breakthrough Action: Practice noticing where you do not feel whole. Note thoughts that would have you feel less than whole. Practice countering those thoughts and replacing them with thoughts in alignment with being whole.

DECLARE: I am worthy.

What is easy for you to believe about this statement?

What makes it hard or difficult?

Where have you heard this?

List all messaging you have encountered around this.

Are you ready to shift?

Breakthrough Question: Why am I worthy?

Breakthrough Action: Practice noticing where you do not feel whole. Note thoughts that would have you feel less than whole. Practice countering those thoughts and replacing them with thoughts in alignment with being whole.

DECLARE: God's plan for me is infinitely better than my plan for me. I come into alignment and accept His plan.

What is easy for you to believe about this statement?

What makes it hard or difficult?

Where have you heard this?

List all messaging you have encountered around this.

Are you ready to shift?

Breakthrough Question: Why is do I come in alignment and accept God's plan for me that is infinitely better than my plan for me?

Breakthrough Action:

DECLARE: I act as though my prayers have already been answered.

What is easy for you to believe about this statement?

What makes it hard or difficult?

Where have you heard this?

List all the messaging you have encountered around this.

Are you ready to shift?

Breakthrough Question: Why do I act as though my prayers have already been answered?

Breakthrough Action: Practice noticing where you do not feel whole. Note thoughts that would have you feel less than whole. Practice countering those thoughts and replacing them with thoughts in alignment with being whole.

DECLARE: _____

What is easy for you to believe about this statement?

What makes it hard or difficult?

Where have you heard this?

List all messaging you have encountered around this.

Are you ready to shift?

Breakthrough Question: Are you willing to let go of any negative messaging around this so you can become the fullest, best version of you?

Breakthrough Action:

Time to Check-In.

You did it! You are working those mental fitness muscles out and will be seeing positive results very soon. Shifting your perspective and digging into why things occur the way they occur for you is challenging—especially when our mental muscles are not accustomed to working out this way.

However, you're doing great!

In the space below, I want you to tell me what you would like to be acknowledged for.

To share, send what you just wrote to our email info@GreatnessRealized.com with the word "Acknowledgement" as the subject line.

CONCLUSION

Congratulations!

What a journey! The areas we covered throughout this book are no doubt fundamental to you realizing every dream that is inside of you. The steps, formulas, and nuggets shared within these pages will absolutely work, if you work at it. However, growth will require you to raise your commitment level to yourself and the amazing vision you have for your life. Thank you for allowing me to work with you and hold this space just for you.

I want to know about your progress! Write to me at info@GreatnessRealized.com with the subject line, "DECLARE" and share your story with me.

If you've finished this book and want more—a deeper dive—go to www.DECLAREGreatness.com and enroll in the DECLARE Greatness course. There, we will break all these concepts down even further and you will have the opportunity to ask specific questions and gain direct answers and results.

For speaking and training inquiries, write to info@GreatnessRealized.com with the subject line, "Speaking & Training" and we will get back to you as soon as possible.

For additional tools and resources visit any one of our sites:

www.GreatnessRealized.com

www.WelcomeReinvention.com

www.DECLAREGreatness.com

www.InstituteforGreatness.com

    It has been my honor to invest in you and pour into your life. I know what can happen to us when we have access and tools that are clearly defined. I believe with all of me that I've provided these points of access for you — that will forever change, alter, and shift the trajectory of your life — propelling you right into the juicy places you know to be possible. I'm cheering for you!

ABOUT THE AUTHOR
WELCOME SARAH

Welcome Sarah is a social entrepreneur, Author, International Speaker, Podcast Host, and Influencer. As the CEO and Founder of the *Greatness Realized* brand of companies, Welcome Sarah has helped thousands of women reinvent their lives, increase their professional influence, and propel their careers forward.

A Native of Kansas City, Missouri, *Welcome Sarah* grew up in a city and family culture that shared strong core tenants of entrepreneurship, education, and philanthropy. She holds a Bachelor of Arts in Organizational Communication with an emphasis in Non-Profit Management from William Jewell College, a Private Liberal Arts College in the heart of the Mid-West and has a Master's Degree in Business Administration.

In 2010, *Welcome Sarah* partnered with *Raven's Hope* to launch an elite multi-national program between the United States and Cambodia that provides education and training to young Cambodian women impacted by human trafficking. Over the past nine years, *Raven's Hope* has helped hundreds of young women become agents of change in Cambodia.

The firm's most recent vertical, *Welcome Reinvention*, is a resource for women who find themselves in transition and reinventing aspects of their lives. The belief at the heart of *Welcome Reinvention* is that no matter the change, transition, or area of reinvention, we thrive when we are clear, with access to tools and exposure diverse environments. *Welcome Reinvention* provides tips and tools in the areas of relationships, business and career, health, and money and finance.

Welcome Sarah is a powerhouse coach, certified by the International Coach Federation. She has a passion for people and impacting lives by creating sustainable shifts where freedom, possibility, and greatness become tangible and realized. When *Welcome Sarah* is not working with women to lean into their purpose, she enjoys traveling, cooking, and spending time with her family.

To learn more, visit www.greatnessrealized.com or www.welcomesarah.com.

Made in the USA
Las Vegas, NV
02 November 2021